American Revolution Stories

Forgotten Tales of Bravery, Betrayal, and Triumph during the Revolutionary War

© Copyright 2023 - All rights reserved.

The content contained within this book may not be reproduced, duplicated, or transmitted without direct written permission from the author or the publisher.

Under no circumstances will any blame or legal responsibility be held against the publisher or author for any damages, reparation, or monetary loss due to the information contained within this book, either directly or indirectly.

Legal Notice:

This book is copyright-protected. It is only for personal use. You cannot amend, distribute, sell, use, quote, or paraphrase any part of the content within this book without the consent of the author or publisher.

Disclaimer Notice:

Please note the information contained within this document is for educational and entertainment purposes only. All effort has been executed to present accurate, up-to-date, reliable, and complete information. No warranties of any kind are declared or implied. Readers acknowledge that the author is not engaging in the rendering of legal, financial, medical, or professional advice. The content within this book has been derived from various sources. Please consult a licensed professional before attempting any techniques outlined in this book.

By reading this document, the reader agrees that under no circumstances is the author responsible for any losses, direct or indirect, that are incurred as a result of the use of the information contained within this document, including, but not limited to, errors, omissions, or inaccuracies.

Table of Contents

INTRODUCTION 1
CHAPTER 1: THE CULPER SPY RING: TALES OF EARLY ESPIONAGE 3
CHAPTER 2: STORIES OF GUERRILLA WARFARE IN THE SOUTH 12
CHAPTER 3: DEBORAH SAMPSON: A WOMAN DISGUISED AS
A SOLDIER 21
CHAPTER 4: DARK DAYS OF THE VALLEY FORGE: STORIES
OF PAIN AND HARDSHIP 30
CHAPTER 5: THE BATTLE OF SARATOGA: TURNING THE TIDE
OF WAR 39
CHAPTER 6: THE MOHAWK VALLEY: TALES OF BETRAYAL AND
LOYALTY ON THE FRONTIER 47
CHAPTER 7: THE TRAITOR'S TREASON: STORIES SURROUNDING
BENEDICT ARNOLD'S BETRAYAL 56
CHAPTER 8: THE BATTLE OF COWPENS: DANIEL MORGAN'S
TACTICAL GENIUS 65
CHAPTER 9: NAVAL WARFARE: JOHN PAUL JONES AND THE
BONHOMME RICHARD 74
CHAPTER 10: THE TREATY OF PARIS: THE PATH TO AMERICAN
INDEPENDENCE 83
CONCLUSION 93
CHECK OUT ANOTHER BOOK IN THE SERIES 95
REFERENCES 96

Introduction

After a decade of growing tensions between the North American colonies and the British government, the British attempts to gain more power over the colonies have proven too much. In the Battles of Lexington and Concord, a clash between the British soldiers and the local militia in 1775 ignited a civil war that entered the history books as the American Revolution (formally known as the American Revolutionary War). The war spread like wildfire from the North to the South, and in three years, it became an international affair when countries like Spain and France joined the American side. After the Continental Navy was established, the war took to the waters, giving even more power to the Americans. Due to the series of missteps and refusal to steer away from old-fashioned tactics on the British side, along with an uncanny ability to capitalize on the enemy's mistakes on the American side, this granted the latter independence. Moreover, the aftermath of this event rewrote the world's political scene by forming new alliances and forcing many forces to reevaluate their connections, along with their leadership and warfare tactics.

While you'll find many books detailing the events of the American Revolution, none are quite like this one! Unlike the others in its category, this book not only provides hard-to-remember historical facts but also delves into the intricacies and the detailed political context of each battle, situation, and maneuver, providing a scenic background of what shaped this period of American history. To offer a fresh perspective on the Revolutionary War and shed light on the multifaceted human experiences that defined the era, this book will unearth lesser-known narratives from the American Revolution, highlighting the often overlooked heroes, complex acts of betrayal, and moments of extraordinary courage that marked the event.

Another great advantage of this book is that it delivers the above in a comprehensive yet easy-to-grasp manner, which makes it an excellent stepping stone for novice history enthusiasts or anyone who wants to learn more about the American Revolution. Whether you are a history teacher looking to spice up your lessons, a researcher, a scholar, or someone who might only learn superficial facts about the event, you won't be disappointed by this book. In it, you'll find everything you need to know about the American Revolutionary War, and by reading it, you will be embarking on a unique journey marked by surprising posts and colorful tales. By the end of your voyage, you will understand the war's historical significance. If you are ready to take this journey and enrich your knowledge about the war that reshaped history, please read on.

Chapter 1: The Culper Spy Ring: Tales of Early Espionage

New York was not always the bustling metropolis it is today, with people all over the world rushing down its streets to make a name for themselves. At one point, the state was a major battleground after America had declared its independence from the colonial rule of the British. The British general, Lord William Howe, captured large parts of the state because of its strategic position, allowing the crown to isolate New England, which was a pillar of revolutionary activity and agitation.

The waterways of New York made the region a brilliant military and commerce hub because supplies could easily be moved around as well as cut off from the enemy by controlling these essential passages. George Washington's terrible defeat in Boston allowed British soldiers to gain control of Manhattan Island. George Washington needed information on how the British were functioning in New York to shift the tides of the war in his favor. This eventually led to the formation of the Culper Spy Ring.

Due to the secretive nature of their activities, history has forgotten many members of the ring. What is known today only came to light centuries after the end of the war in the 1930s. Although many people who served as spies were not honored in their time, organizations today acknowledge their contributions and the pivotal role they played in winning America its independence.

How the Culper Spy Ring Was Formed

The Culper Ring was formed after George Washington's attempts at espionage failed.
https://commons.wikimedia.org/wiki/File:Gilbert_Stuart_Williamstown_Portrait_of_George_Washington.jpg

Before the Culper Ring was formed, George Washington's earlier attempts at espionage resulted in deadly failures. However, these blunders laid the foundation for what would become one of the most successful spy rings. When George Washington gave notice that he was recruiting spies to monitor military activity in New York, he jumped at the opportunity. Hale became legendary for uttering a timeless classic, with his last words being the inspiringly patriotic quote, "I only regret that I have but one life to give to my country."

On September 15, 1776, Nathan Hale entered British-controlled New York in disguise as a schoolmaster. The Yale graduate was well-suited to play this role brilliantly. Hale meticulously gathered notes but was unfortunately caught and executed. Nathan Hale already had a passion for his country, fighting under the banner of Lt. Col. Thomas

Knowlton's Rangers. When George Washington reached out to recruit members of the Rangers for spying activities, they all declined, not out of cowardice but more out of pride because they refused to die out of uniform. Furthermore, spying at the time was not seen as honorable. Amazingly, Nathan Hale, who was the only Ranger to respond to Washington's request, let his love for his country push him beyond the negative opinions of his peers by making the disrespected decision to go undercover behind enemy lines.

The tragic failure that Nathan Hale suffered prompted George Washington to develop more sophisticated and less dangerous ways of spying. One of those innovations of spying that was developed after the death of Nathan Hale was using patriots who were not service people to gather information. Using military men made it easier for spies to be identified, so the strategy of using civilians was crucial for gathering essential information that shifted many battles. From the miscalculation of Hale, better espionage was developed because for the entire five years that the Culper Ring operated in Long Island and New York City, nobody was discovered. Even when members of the ring were arrested, the true identities and functioning of the brave spies were never unveiled.

Since spying was not yet built into the strategies of war in a meaningful way, many of the Ring's members had to develop methods and techniques in the line of duty. Using technology and code words changed how espionage was previously done. Without the formation of the Culper Ring and the piles of intelligence they provided, the war may not have ended in favor of Washington. Therefore, the Culper Ring's often-forgotten role in the war must be highlighted because it was instrumental in the establishment of a free, non-colonial nation that would grow to become the superpower that the United States is now.

With military personnel spread thin and the risk of a repeat of what happened to Nathan Hale occurring, Washington had no option but to make use of civilians who had sympathy for his independence fight. Like many other great inventions, the Culper Ring was born out of necessity. George Washington would not be able to make any strategic moves without information about the colonial enemy. Washington was hyper-aware of the need for intelligence... so much that he constantly pressured the Culper Ring to provide more information, even though their spying efforts had yielded more usable data than any other group on either side.

The Role of Benjamin Tallmadge

Benjamin Tallmadge was a central figure in setting up the Culper Ring. When Washington realized the necessity for accurate and usable intel and the dangers of spy work, he knew that good leadership and planning was the only way for their espionage to be successful. Therefore, Washington appointed Tallmadge as the director of military intelligence, making him responsible for the operations the ring would undertake in New York.

Tallmadge, understanding the sensitivity and importance of the task at hand, only recruited people he trusted, including his school friends, Austin Roe, Abraham Woodhull, Anna Strong, and Caleb Brewster. Other members, like Sarah Townsend, were later introduced. Tallmadge was the one who realized it was a lot more effective to send civilians on reconnaissance missions because they could easily fly under the radar without garnering much attention. He also utilized women in his missions because British troops were typically on the lookout for men. Tallmadge has been credited with being the first spymaster in America. Although Nathan Hale was Tallmadge's close friend from their days at Yale, Hale's death while working on gathering intelligence in the field may have been what drove Tallmadge's commitment. With his new approach to spying, Tallmadge was successful where Hale had failed.

Tallmadge was a master tactician, using systems like numerical code names to hide the identities of his informants and other key players involved. There were 763 total combinations of numbers used to refer to different people or places. For example, 745 was England, 727 was New York, and 711 was George Washington. They also used codenames like "John Bolton," which referred to Tallmadge. Washington had a close relationship with Tallmadge and knew his knowledge of the region made him well-suited for their covert activities.

Tallmadge was the main line of communication informing Washington about all the key military operations in New York. Their correspondence was letters written in code to make it impossible for enemies to decipher their plans if the written notes were discovered. Tallmadge organized the team and established the complex systems that the Culper Ring would use to keep their activities under wraps from the British authorities. The information transmitted by Tallmadge would shift events in the Revolutionary War. One instance when the intelligence that Tallmadge and his team had collected was used by

Washington was when General Henry Clinton planned an expedition to Rhode Island. Tallmadge's early warnings about the general's plans allowed Washington to station troops, which prevented Clinton's planned attack.

In many ways, Tallmadge was the centerpiece of the operation, acting as a middleman between Washington and the field agents. This position was extremely dangerous, but Tallmadge's carefulness ensured that everyone, including himself, was kept safe, managing to avoid capture. The spying techniques spearheaded by Tallmadge were so good that the British began taking their spying more seriously as well by unleashing more agents out into the field. Washington trusted Tallmadge with this dangerous role because he had valiantly fought in numerous battles in the north during his time in service.

How Tallmadge recruited the first members of the team showed how cautious and vigilant the leader was. Abraham Woodhull was Tallmadge's childhood friend, whom he had known for years. Along with Caleb Brewster, he was one of the first people whom Tallmadge recruited. Tallmadge knew that the secretive game he was playing could easily be disrupted by any weak link. He had to make sure that everybody aware of the sensitive information was fully committed to the cause. Any leak would undoubtedly result in military interventions from the British, which could completely destabilize the revolution.

Benjamin Tallmadge would be rewarded for his efforts with a job that was just as difficult as the spy work he had left behind when the war ended. Tallmadge served in the U.S. House of Representatives and died peacefully from old age when he was 81. The credit that President George Washington got for orchestrating many key battles and plans in the Revolutionary War was well-deserved, but people who served under him – like Tallmadge – are just as much responsible for the victories that the Continental Army savored.

Key Operatives within the Culper Spy Ring

Many courageous people formed the Culper Spy Ring, and all positively contributed to ensuring that the war would be won in the long run. Due to the secrecy of the collective, many of the network names are lost to history, but the roles and operations of a few central figures are still known today. Abraham Woodhull was one of the first recruits by the pseudonym Samuel Culper Sr., and Robert Townsend went by Samuel

Culper Jr., which is why the group was described as the "Culper" spy ring.

The ring worked like a well-oiled machine, deceiving the British at every turn with its cunningness. Abraham Woodhull traveled back and forth from New York, collecting information about crucial military actions like naval maneuvers. Dispatches were then given to Caleb Brewster, who would take the treacherous journey of delivering these messages to Connecticut. Benjamin Tallmadge would then receive the messages and give them to General George Washington himself. The close bond of trust between Washington and Tallmadge is why the operations of the spy ring were so rock solid.

The work of the Culper Spy Ring was dangerous and life-threatening because any action taken against the crown would be seen as treason, which carried with it the death penalty. The constant pressure of being discovered weighed heavily on Woodhall, and he needed some assistance. This justified paranoia that Woodhall experienced led him to recruit Robert Townsend, who was a successful and connected merchant.

Austin Roe was a tavern keeper who helped courier messages to Manhattan. His business venture gave him the perfect excuse to always be on the move without raising any suspicion. Roe's neighbor was a woman named Anna Strong. She had already suffered because of the war, with her husband, Patriot Judge Selah Strong, being imprisoned on a British ship called the HMS Jersey in 1778. Some historians consider Selah Strong to be a part of the ring, but he was imprisoned during many of its operations.

Later on, Selah Strong also served as part of the U.S. House of Representatives in New York. His arrest was for a crime similar to spying and for providing information against the crown to the revolutionary cause, but because he was not a military member, the British government did not consider him a spy. The Culper Spy Ring helped evolve the thinking of what a spy meant due to them recruiting civilians. Ana String would hang clothes on her washing line that signaled Brewster where to meet with Woodhull. This was before they managed to get more sophisticated communication methods.

One of the greatest achievements of the spy ring was that it helped solidify the relationship between the French army and the American Revolutionary movement. In 1780, the British drafted plans to ambush troops from the French, which had just touched down on American shores. The attack was supposed to take place in Rhode Island, but the surprise attack was thwarted because of intelligence gathered by the operatives of the Culper Spy Ring. Another major discovery credited to the ring was the treasonous actions of America's most hated backstabber, Benedict Arnold. The spy ring uncovered communication between Benedict Arnold and the Chief Intelligence Officer for the British, John Andre, who worked under General Henry Clinton. Arnold planned to give control of a fort at West Point to the British forces. Upon the plan being revealed, John Andre was captured and executed on direct orders from General George Washington.

The Culper Spy Ring operated successfully, without any arrests, for five years, from 1777 to 1783. During this time, they were able to get a lot of intelligence to Washington, who would use it to strategize for battles. It can be argued that without the hard work of the spy ring, America would not have won the Revolutionary War. The information provided by the spies included everything from British plans in New York and the surrounding areas to details about military fortifications, as well as the movement of military forces throughout the region. Without this information, Washington would have been blind to the advanced and battle-hardened British forces. The Revolutionary War served to highlight how important gathering intelligence was for swaying the outcomes of battles and drawing up plans that could catch the enemy off guard.

Methods and Techniques Employed by the Culper Spy Ring

The British had already developed complex codes through their imperial conquests. The British military also had scores of highly-trained cryptographers who developed and decoded hidden messages for Britain's military correspondence. Because of this, when the ring was being established, they had to quickly develop codes that their members could easily learn. Basic codes were created that used techniques like swapping out certain letters with specialized symbols that only readers who were informed about the code could understand. They also made use of code names and numbers to hide the identities of the people involved. Some of the team members were so careful that they refused to reveal their identities to George Washington in case he was captured –

or if someone near him was a spy who would reveal their identities to the British. Being exposed was a huge concern because they lived and traveled between British-controlled territories.

Both sides were already using crude versions of invisible ink, made with materials like lemon juice, which could be heated up to reveal the true message. General George Washington recognized the ineffectiveness of such methods because, with a simple flame, the enemies would know the details of your most secretive plans. Washington wrote a letter to Elias Boudinot, highlighting the need for an invisible ink that did not respond to fire but rather to liquor being rubbed on it. Following this appeal from Washington, Sir James Jay created an invisible ink that would only be revealed when a certain liquid chemical compound was rubbed on it. The ingredients to develop this ink were scarce, so they were only able to produce it in small batches at a time. Washington received a reminder of how important concealing your correspondence in code or invisible ink was when letters between him and Tallmadge were intercepted, resulting in the arrest of his spy, George Higday, and nearly causing the Culper Spy Ring to collapse. However, the ring managed to persist through this hiccup without getting exposed.

Tallmadge was instrumental in creating many of the spying techniques that the ring used, but Washington's brilliance as a spymaster also shined through. Washington not only emphasized the importance of gathering information but also began a campaign of misinformation in order to disrupt the intelligence that the British gathered. For example, in 1775, Washington's troops were dealing with a gunpowder shortage in Massachusetts, so they needed armies to deliver more of it to them. While they waited, they could not let the British know about this weakness, so Washington ordered them to fill some gunpowder barrels up with sand so it would look like they were well-equipped. Another masterful use of misinformation was when Washington organized troops in small groups scattered over wide areas so that the British believed he had more personnel than there actually were.

The use of invisible ink, misinformation, and coded letters were the intelligence tools that helped secure America's victory in the Revolutionary War. Furthermore, using women and unnoticeable civilians instead of military operatives helped prevent the discovery of spies, particularly those who operated as part of the Culper Spy Ring. Their network of complex, interlocking moving parts kept the British guessing and revealed intel that culminated in many winning strategies across numerous battles. Although the spy ring was forgotten for many years, only getting rediscovered in the 1930s, and many names of operatives are still a mystery, the important role that members of this collective played hugely contributed to the American cause... so much so that they could not have won the war without their help.

Chapter 2: Stories of Guerrilla Warfare in the South

The Revolutionary War was a military and political struggle that shaped American history. Tension arose after the British started taxing American colonies. They realized they couldn't stay under the control of the British much longer, which led to one of the biggest wars America had witnessed. The Americans decided to change their destiny and fight for their independence. It was the first revolutionary war in modern history where people demanded constitutional rights, popular sovereignty, and the rule of law.

This chapter provides an overview of the American Revolution, the significance of the Southern Theater, and the story of guerrilla warfare.

The Revolutionary War

During the 17th and 18th centuries, the Americans lived in peace under British rule. The American colonies governed themselves in the way that they elected their assembly, but the crown government chose the governors. The colonies flourished, and the British economy prospered as well. Both regions lived in harmony; however, things were about to take a turn.

After the war with the Indians and the French, Britain found itself in great debt. In 1763, Britain issued a law to raise taxes in American colonies. They believed this was fair since they defended the colonies against the Indians and the French. However, the Americans didn't share the same view. The colonies realized they had no choice but to fight for their independence.

The war lasted for eight years and ended with the British defeat. Many factors contributed to America's victory, like the French, who provided them with arms and supplies, as well as the Southern Theater. During the war's final years, the South played a huge role that changed its course.

During the first three years of the war, most of the battles took place in the north... in Philadelphia, New York, and Boston. However, after America's victory in the battle of Saratoga, the British decided to head to the South. They believed there were more loyalists in the Southern colonies, so they would garner more support there. They thought capturing the South would be easier, and once they finished, they could return to the north. However, they were in for a surprise.

British Commander Sir Henry Clinton tried to secure his country's status by capturing Charleston, one of the most significant cities in the South. However, he failed, so he shifted his attention to Savannah, which his army captured in 1778.

In 1779, Clinton made an unprecedented decree that would grant freedom to all enslaved people who escaped from their American patriot masters. The British aim was to destroy the rebels' economy and to have the enslaved people join the British army and serve as soldiers, servants, nurses, or cooks.

In 1780, Clinton took an army of 14,000 men and tried to capture Charleston again. This time, the Americans were heavily outnumbered. American Major General Benjamin Lincoln had no choice but to surrender, with 5,000 soldiers, marking the most significant loss for the Americans in the Revolutionary War.

British general Colonel Banastre Tarleton pursued the rest of the colonials in the South. They caught Abraham Buford's Continentals. Although they tried to surrender, Tarleton killed many of them. However, this story is debatable as some believe it didn't happen.

Clinton issued a proclamation that all Patriots must pledge allegiance to the crown. He then handed the South's command to Charles Lord Cornwallis and left for New York. After the fall of Charleston and the Americans' huge loss, the British were close to controlling the South.

However, after the massacre of the Americans at the hands of Tarleton and Clinton's ill-received proclamation, the rebel militias, under the command of Francis Marion, refused to give up to the British and insisted on reclaiming the South.

Francis Marion, the "Swamp Fox," and His Leadership in Guerrilla Warfare

Marion wasn't one of the 5,000 soldiers who accompanied Lincoln in Charleston, as he was recovering from a broken ankle. He became the leader of the militia in Charleston after Lincoln's colossal loss. Although the Patriots didn't have enough men or equipment to face the British, this didn't stop Marion from making a move.

Marion resorted to techniques where he would surprise enemies from behind.
https://commons.wikimedia.org/wiki/File:Francis_Marion_001.jpg

In August 1780, Marion took 50 men and raided the British. They hid among the plants and attacked the soldiers from behind in order to rescue 150 American men and capture 20 British soldiers. This was called the guerilla tactic. Since Marion didn't have enough men or resources to go into battle with the British, he resorted to these techniques where he would surprise his enemies from behind. Marion didn't believe in destroying his enemies... he wanted to weaken them until they were unable to fight. Destroying the British army was impossible since they were extremely powerful, and the Patriots were no match for them. Marion's tactics were straightforward and simple, and they managed to shake the British army.

This was an embarrassing defeat for the British, who realized they weren't in total control of the South as they had initially perceived. As a result, they couldn't return to the north.

Encouraged by his big victory, Marion continued attacking the British with his guerilla tactics. He achieved one victory after another, and the British began to consider him a serious threat. Since he was cunning in his attacks, they never knew where he would strike, which gave him a great advantage. The British then divided their forces, hoping they would either find him or weaken him.

Marion became a local hero. He not only gave the Americans hope that they could win this war, but he also treated his enemy with compassion. While many American and British leaders punished their enemies by hanging them, killing their livestock, and burning their homes, Marion refrained from those horrendous acts. Even though he couldn't prevent his subordinates from this cruel behavior, he would discourage it and report it to his commanding officer.

On September 4th, Marion and 53 of his men hid in an open swale and surprised and defeated a group of 250 Tory forces. Marion divided his men so they would cover more ground. They attacked 45 horsemen and disrupted the rest of them, leading many to hide in the swamps. The Tories were furious and humiliated. They took it out on the Patriots by destroying their farms and burning their homes.

The British kept sending Tory militias to fight Marion and his men. The news of one of the British militia reached Marion. It was a group of 200 men who were under the command of Colonel Samuel Tynes. Upon hearing the name, Marion was adamant about fighting the militia, even though he only had 150 men. Tynes was a traitor... he used to be a Patriot but established an alliance with the British; therefore, this was Marion's chance to punish him for his betrayal.

Marion and his men attacked the Tories when they were sleeping and killed 43 British men while the rest escaped to the swamps. The

Americans confiscated their supplies, horses, and ammunition.

The British weren't happy with Marion's series of victories. Cornwallis sent word to Tarleton to bring troops from Pennsylvania and New York to Charleston. Tarleton and his troops went after Marion and his men, which turned into a cat-and-mouse game. After Tarleton spent days chasing Marion, he turned the tables and chased the British. Tarleton and his men hid in the swamps. He even admitted that he failed to capture Marion by saying that the devil himself (referring to himself, Tarleton) couldn't catch the old fox (referring to Marion). This was how Marion earned the nickname the "Swamp Fox."

Interestingly, no one ever used this nickname when Marion was alive. It was first mentioned in his biography, which was published after his death.

In December 1780, Nathaniel Greene became the commander of the American South forces. He was in charge of a poorly-equipped, small army that couldn't withstand a battle against the British, so Greene decided to seek Marion's help. He knew that Marion was his only hope against Cornwallis and his men.

In 1781, Marion was running his operations from Snow Island. He worked with Lieutenant Henry Lee, who, in spite of their constant arguments, had a close relationship.

Marion showed the British his true power when he tried to take back Georgetown. Even though they failed, it became clear to the British that Marion was more powerful than they had ever imagined. After Tarleton's failure, Cornwallis sent Colonel John Watson Tadwell-Watson after Marion.

Watson's fellow officers disliked him, so none of them joined him on the mission. He took 300 infantry, 150 cavalry, and 20 dragoons to fight the Swamp Fox and his men. Watson and Marion finally came face to face. Marion was outnumbered and under-equipped. He had no choice but to trick the British in order to gain the advantage. He pulled his forces back so that Watson believed he was retreating. The British followed him but quickly realized that this was a trick.

The Americans charged, but the British quickly counterattacked. This led to the Bridges Campaign Battle, which lasted for two weeks. Marion and his soldiers outsmarted the British. Watson only wanted Marion, so he left his post to chase after him; however, he couldn't catch him, and Marion escaped from the British once more.

Marion kept attacking the British and weakening their defenses. In one ambush, he managed to cause 100 casualties while only losing four of his men.

In September 1781, Marion's soldiers joined Greene's army to fight the British in a battle. Marion also played a huge role as he was the commander of 700 militiamen. The Americans were advancing while the British fell behind.

The Americans seized a large quantity of alcohol, and they started drinking. The British took advantage of their enemies' intoxicated state and counterattacked. This turned into a bloody battle with severe losses on both sides. Although the British held the field, they were far too weak to keep going. So, who won the battle? Well, each side claimed they did. However, the one thing everyone knew for a fact was that Marion and his men performed very well. Without them, the American army would have perished.

On October 19th, 1781, the Americans won and took control of the South.

Who Was Francis Marion?

On February 26, 1732, Marion was born on his parent's Gabriel and Esther Marion plantation in Berkeley County, South Carolina. He was the youngest of six siblings and a very restless child. When he turned six, his family moved to St. George, where he and his siblings attended school.

When he turned 15, he got the taste of his first adventure when he joined the crew of a schooner. A whale struck the ship, and it sank. The crew spent seven days on a lifeboat trying to get to the shore, but sadly, two of them died. This experience was traumatizing for the young boy, and ever since, Marion stayed away from the water. He spent the next few years working on his parents' plantation.

At the age of 25, he joined the militia and fought in the French and Indian War. He was an exceptional soldier and managed to rise quickly through the ranks. When he became a lieutenant, he fought against the Cherokees. He learned a lot from them, like ambushing, concealment, and utilizing terrain, which influenced his guerrilla tactics. In 1761, he returned home and decided to buy a plantation, which he did in 1773.

In 1775, he became the captain of his own regiment in South Carolina. He was tasked to build a fort in Charleston. After building the fort, he faced the British in the Battle of Sullivan Island and defeated their men. As a result, he was promoted to lieutenant colonel. He spent three years in South Carolina, which gave him immense knowledge of the region.

One time, he was at a dinner party where everyone was drinking heavily except for Marion, who wasn't much of a drinker. To escape the intoxication, he left the party by jumping out of the window and breaking his ankle. He couldn't participate with Lincoln's men; however, he managed to free the 150 Americans while he was still injured and unable to walk.

Marion was a great leader, and his soldiers were ready to follow him to the end of the world. They were even called "Marion's men," and they served without pay.

Marion became an American hero, and the movie The Patriot, starring Mel Gibson, was loosely based on his life.

The Southern Theater in the Revolutionary War

During the second half of the Revolutionary War, the Southern Theater was the center of military operations. Many strategic battles took place in the South, and it was where the Americans first tried the guerilla tactics that changed the face of warfare forever.

In 1777 and 1778, Britain found itself in a weak position. After their defeat in the Battle of Saratoga, the north colonies signed a treaty with the French. The British realized that they might have to go to war with France, so they changed their strategy. Instead of fighting the Continental Army, whom the French aided, they decided to eliminate the Patriots, the majority of whom lived in the South.

The British had a few victories when they first arrived in the South. They managed to capture Georgia, Savannah, and Charleston. However, the British and the Americans faced a few challenges there. A civil war broke out between the Loyalists and the Patriots, leading to the division of the South. The British were also fighting battles with the Patriot militias. The British thought that the loyalists had a more extensive influence in the South. However, after their arrival, many Americans joined the Patriots and were ready to fight for their independence.

The British also faced their biggest challenge when they tried to capture Charleston for the first time, but they failed to reduce Fort Sullivan. The Americans also encountered a few challenges. The South depended on agriculture, and there weren't many factories to manufacture weapons and other equipment for the soldiers. The South was also divided and didn't have the support of the French, so they struggled to defeat the British on multiple occasions.

However, things changed with Marion, Greene, and American soldier Daniel Morgan, who resorted to guerilla warfare, which gave them the advantage that contributed to their victory.

What Is Guerrilla Warfare?

Guerrilla warfare involves surprise raids, ambushes, and unconventional styles of combat. It was known for being savage, disorganized, and chaotic. Many soldiers preferred the guerilla warfare technique since it gave them more freedom than conventional techniques.

Guerrilla warfare is different from other war techniques since it focuses on mobility, sabotage, and hit-and-run tactics. Conventional war techniques, on the other hand, focus on artillery, infantry, air forces, and armor. Guerrilla warfare played a considerable role in the Revolutionary War. While it didn't directly contribute to the American victory, it slowed down the British and prolonged the war. By the end, the British had exhausted all their resources, and the soldiers were beaten and tired, leading to the American's victory.

Marion's guerilla warfare techniques depended on undercover and sneaky tactics. They hid in and escaped through swamps. He and his men would also hide in the woods of the backcountry in order to surprise and raid their enemies. He often attacked his enemies from behind to catch them off guard and confuse them. The British were always on high alert because of Marion and his men's surprise moves. However, he managed to surprise them every time. The use of hit-and-run tactics disrupted the British supply line. Ambushes also overwhelmed the enemy, which made them constantly tired and prone to making mistakes.

Hit-and-run tactics depend on launching short and surprise attacks and then quickly withdrawing so the enemy doesn't have a chance to respond. Marion used this technique on multiple occasions, which prevented him from facing or engaging with the British army.

Marion managed to attack the British multiple times and escape before they knew what hit them. Seeing that in one battle, he only lost four men while his enemy lost 100, this technique was proven to be very effective, and to this day, people all over the world still use it.

The Revolutionary War is a lesson in patriotism and what a person is willing to do for their country. Marion couldn't wait for his ankle to heal and go after the British. He was outnumbered and didn't have enough weapons, yet he used his intelligence and kept defeating them at every turn. The Americans experienced many losses, including thousands of men, yet they never gave up and believed they would eventually win their homes back.

In spite of being in the middle of a war, Marion refused to let the British citizens pay for their army's mistakes, so he exercised patience and compassion. One could learn this great lesson from Marion: *vengeance is never the answer.*

Chapter 3: Deborah Sampson: A Woman Disguised as a Soldier

Conflicts often happen when people show their true colors. Those are the times when the real patriots emerge... when people with big words and small actions are challenged. Many fantasize about historical events, wondering what they would have done had they been in those situations. Would you fight and stand up for what's right? Would you cower or turn the other cheek? Would you run for your life, and if so, would you save your loved ones? Perhaps you would have stood your ground, swearing to water the earth with your own blood before you move an inch.

The role of women in historical revolutions and wars is often overlooked. They are mostly confined within stereotypical frames, painting them in a helpless manner and waiting at home for their male counterparts to return and save them. Maybe they take part in nursing the wounded, cooking for the soldiers, or knitting their war attire. However, ever so often, a figure emerges, breaking the walls of the traditional compartmentalization of females. A fierce warrior chooses to put down the knitting kit, pick up the musket, and charge the enemy lines.

Deborah Sampson proved she could defend her rights and freedom the same way a man could.
https://commons.wikimedia.org/wiki/File:DeborahSampson.jpg

Deborah Samson is one of those few brave souls who took a chance and proved she could defend her rights and freedom in the same manner as a man could. Like most other prominent female figures, the tale of Sampson's courage has been swept under the rug for far too long. With little information available regarding the circumstances that led to her enlisting in the army, some scholars resolved to speculate on missing parts. That was until her neighbor's journals (Abner Weston) were unearthed, shedding some light on some of the obscure parts of her life.

Who Is Deborah Sampson?

Deborah Sampson Gannett entered the world with great fanfare on December 17, 1760, in Plympton, Massachusetts. Born to Deborah (Bradford) Sampson and Jonathan Sampson Jr., she was one of seven siblings. Her parents were descended directly from Priscilla Alden and Jonathan, two illustrious pilgrims. William Bradford, the governor of Massachusetts, was related to Sampson.

Sampson had a rough childhood and adolescence. She came from an honorable family, but the family battled to make ends meet due to financial difficulties. The rest of the story is a wild guess as to what happened to her father. While some academics claim that the family patriarch deserted them, others think he just never came back after a sea journey, possibly being lost at sea.

The impoverished family was forced into making some harsh decisions. Deborah's mother came to the conclusion that it would be in the best interest of her children if they were reallocated to separate households, possibly relatives. As the child grew and started to become a burden to her foster guardians, she was subjected to yet another kind of hardship. At the young age of ten, little Deborah was forced to serve as an indentured servant to the family of Deacon Benjamin Thomas until she reached the legal age of 18. He was a farmer who hailed from Middleborough with a huge family. In exchange for her services to the family, she was given food, shelter, and clothing.

During her years with the family, Sampson absorbed their personal, patriotic political views and adopted them as her own. She was also free to self-educate and explore the world through the books offered to her at the home where she served. Believing in the power of education and literacy, the Deacon allowed her to attend classes with his boys. Regular farm tasks, including woodworking, stacking hay, plowing the fields, spreading fertilizer, and milking cows, also helped her acquire a wealth of other physical abilities.

After completing her contracted years, she set off to become a teacher between the years 1779 and 1780. In the harsh winters, she worked as a weaver, and she tended to her own sheep and chickens. That was until she decided to take a more serious stance to serve her country.

The Revolutionary War had been raging since 1776, when Sampson was just 16 years old, and women were not permitted to serve as soldiers in the army. Seeking adventure and wanting to leave a deep impact on the world, Deborah had other plans. She didn't want to simply become a cook or a nurse; she had higher aspirations than that, so she took matters into her own hands. Sampson made up a story of having to accept a new and better teaching position. She promptly stitched up her own military uniform, complete with a coat, a waistcoat, and breeches, and headed toward the front lines.

Some tales suggest that it wasn't just patriotism that encouraged Sampson to take up arms. It is believed that money also played a factor in her decision. During the diminishing years of the war, when towns couldn't fill their recruitment quotas, bounties were offered to raise the number of volunteer soldiers.

It was a habit of some to sign up for the army, wait to get paid, and then desert their positions. They would then move on to another location, sign up again, and repeat the cycle to receive more bounties.

The Birth of Robert Shurtliff

Aged 21, Deborah moved swiftly to enlist in the army and serve her country. Knowing that there was no way a male-dominated army would consent to her joining their ranks, she decided to disguise herself in male clothing and use the fake alias of "Robert Shurtliff." Later on, it was discovered that this name was of her deceased brother. It is said that she made an initial attempt to join the army near Middleborough, though she never admitted to it, while others seemed to have clear memories of the incident. She was staying with Benjamin Leonard's family when she decided to borrow one of his son's (Samuel) suits. As she entered the recruitment office, she declared herself as "Timothy Thayer." However, the ruse came to a halt when a woman recognized her as she was exiting a tavern with a group of soldiers despite her wearing her soldier's uniform.

She was then forced to return the bounty she had not spent, pay damages, and was banned from the local recruiting office. Her actions led to her excommunication from the Baptist Church of Middleborough, citing one of the main reasons being that she wore men's clothes. Embarrassed by the outcome of her attempt, she thought it best to leave Middleborough for good. This led to her second try, which had a much more rewarding result.

Before her 2nd attempt, she wandered for about a month at the seaport in New Bradford. After that, she headed to Boston with plans of becoming a cabin boy. However, after a few attempts, she couldn't find a good captain or a proper bounty. She continued westward until she arrived at a village called Bellingham. There, she met an army recruiter desperate to fill a quota for a town nearby called Uxbridge. Satisfied with the bounty offered, Private Robert Shurtliff was born.

By May of 1782, Sampson had traveled to Worcester, Mass, to enlist in Captain Webb's company of light infantry in the 4th Massachusetts Regiment of the Continental Army. This troop happened to be one of the most active troops in Hudson Valley between the years 1782 and 1783. The light infantry gained that name for a number of reasons. The soldiers within the company had to be 5'5", with enough physical endurance to maintain a fast and steady pace. They were also known for carrying fewer supplies than most and taking part in smaller, precarious missions and tussles.

Deborah's physical vigor from working long years on a farm, along with her boyish features, were key factors in her success in hiding her true identity. Sampson stood at 5 feet and 8 inches tall. She was heavy-boned, with a long, narrow face and blonde locks, which she cut short before enlisting. Other soldiers often teased her because they thought she was simply a teenage boy who could not grow a beard. The other soldiers even went so far as to call Sampson "the blooming boy" or "Molly." The chances of being discovered were slight at the time. This was due to the fact that personal hygiene was not a priority during that period, so soldiers didn't bathe very often, and they mostly slept in their uniforms.

She also tried to change the way she looked by flattening her chest with a tightly wrapped cloth. She lied when one of the soldiers asked her why she knew how to sew, saying that it was because her family didn't have any females that she had to learn.

She and the other five troops had to sleep in a tent. She waited until nighttime to use the outdoor restroom and changed clothes in the shadows so she wouldn't be discovered. Sampson worked very hard to conceal her identity. She sustained injuries in a battle that took place in Tarrytown, Westchester County, just north of New York. She had a deep gash from either a blow or a knife to her head and a bullet (in some stories, two bullets) to the thigh. In an attempt to keep her identity concealed, she only allowed the medic to treat the blow to her head. She then snuck out of the tent and proceeded to remove the pistol bullet from her thigh by using a pen knife and a sewing needle, completely unassisted.

In another instance, as she took part in a skirmish facing loyalist raiders, otherwise known as cowboys, Deborah sustained a gunshot injury to the shoulder.

Instead of seeking a physician's support to remove the foreign object, it is said that she just left the musket ball in her shoulder and continued on with her duties in an effort to remain hidden.

Even though Deborah had boyish features that assisted her in concealing herself as a soldier, as a man, she was quite attractive. The camp was periodically visited by women who found her charming, a predicament that she maneuvered through by politely letting them down gently.

Her Time in Service

Deborah proved her value to the army, leading to them assigning her several high-risk missions that included spying, scouting, and performing raids. Sampson was no stranger to cannons firing at her, and she did not shy away from leading expeditions with the continental army, which usually resulted in victories. She was a superb marksman and served with the rangers, a unique branch of the light infantry that participated in scouting and surveillance operations in addition to fighting mostly on foot.

During her service, she was tasked with the dangerous mission of scouting in neutral territories to assess the British build-up of soldiers and equipment in Manhattan, New York. In an attempt to purge the Tories in the East Chester area, her regiment was dispatched to West Point, New York. Despite the revolution, Tories were colonists who stuck with the United Kingdom. They were known to cause trouble around the area of New York in favor of their allegiances.

There is some confusion regarding how she and a fellow soldier, who went by the name Richard Snow, were detained by a Tori in a stifling hot attic. The Tory, who was called Abraham Van Tassel, kept them there in his house until Snow, who was sick at the time, could not handle the confinement and died.

In June 1782, Sampson, accompanied by two other sergeants, led a group of 30 infantrymen in a confrontation against the Tories. The fight ended with Sampson claiming her revenge for Snow's death and the capture of 15 men. During the siege of Yorktown, she was said to have participated in digging trenches and enduring heavy cannon fire.

She and her companions arrived at Fort Ticonderoga in November of 1782. There, she faced out against Native Americans who were backing the Tories in the hopes that they would eventually assist them in regaining their lost territories. General John Paterson was aware of Sampson's upbeat and enthusiastic demeanor. By April of 1783, Sampson had been promoted to serve as the general's personal assistant, also known as the general's aide. Her duties included wiping his boots, polishing his swords, organizing his clothes, preparing his meals, and running a variety of errands for him. She received a modest room to herself and a feather bed in exchange.

Not long afterward, General George Washington made the declaration "Cessation of Hostilities between the United States of America and the King of Great Britain." Sampson wasn't sure how she felt about this announcement. She was worried that the end of the war would mean her return to her old life.

The Secret Was Out

As the war neared its end, Sampson was stationed with her military unit in Philadelphia. The mission was to fight off a rebellion led by some American officers as part of a mop-up operation. What Sampson didn't count on was Malaria. She was struck by a fever so harsh that there were talks among funeral planners about where to take her body. Drifting between consciousness and unconsciousness, she had little control over who had access to her body. However, fate would have it that Dr. Barnabas Binney would treat her. While treating the ailing young soldier, the doctor discovered her true gender but decided to keep the matter under wraps. He only revealed the true identity of Deborah to another female who was tending to the wounded and was instructed to keep the secret to herself.

After regaining her consciousness, the good doctor had Sampson transport her to his own home, where she was tended to by his family, specifically his niece. When she had fully recovered, she headed back to the line of duty with General Paterson. A popular belief states that before she left, doctor Binney wrote a letter to the general revealing her true gender, and he asked her to deliver it. When Deborah handed the letter to the general, he seemed more shocked than angered. The records of several soldiers present, as well as that of the generals, suggested that he handled the news with grace and composure. Instead of suffering severe consequences for her deception, the young soldier received an honorable discharge from the Continental Army by General Henry Knox and Commander-in-Chief George Washington.

Her time in the army ended in October of 1783.

Sampan was discharged and went to work as a farm hand on her uncle's farm in Stoughton, Massachusetts, before moving to Boston. It wasn't until the spring of 1784 that she began wearing skirts once more; up until then, she wore men's clothing and portions of her army outfit.

In April of 1784, Deborah wedded Benjamin Gannett, a farmhand from Sharon, Massachusetts. She gave birth to three children – two daughters and one son, who later became a soldier, not unlike his mother.

Her experience was first published under the title "The Female Review" in 1797. Later, in 1802, Deborah engaged a writer to compose a speech about her life.

As a veteran, she had the right to claim back pay and pension. She made a request that was approved by the Massachusetts legislature and Governor John Hancock. The back pay was approved with interest. She received a full military pension after her friend and patriot, Paul Revere, used his influence to convince those in power to pay her what she was owed. Paul Revere gained notoriety when he alerted the soldiers to the approaching British forces by riding his horse all the way from Boston to Lexington and Concord, Massachusetts. Sampson was also granted a piece of land by the American Congress.

The pension she received was $4 as compensation for being an injured soldier while on duty. With the help of this money, she and her family were able to purchase a home and landscape their own land. The pension was doubled in 1818. The family got by, but not by much. At times, Deborah would try to increase the family's income by teaching at a schoolhouse nearby.

On occasion, she was requested to attend events and give lectures about her time in the army. Sampson was more than happy to oblige and had no problem adding little exaggerated factoids to her stories to make them more interesting. She famously called herself the American Heroine. She is also considered the first female lecturer in the history of the United States of America.

Deborah Sampson Gannett passed away on April 29th, 1827, at the age of 68. She was buried near her home, with her headstone reading, "The Female Soldier." Her husband, Benjamin, pleaded with the American congress to grant him a continuation of his wife's pension. However, this was unlikely to pass since, at the time, there were no laws in place to grant widows the pensions of their deceased husbands, let alone widowers.

In 1836, the widower made another appeal that led to Congress passing the act. He then provided proof that his wife's battle injuries had cost the family 600 dollars over the years. By that time, the family had been rendered poor and in dire need of any financial aid.

After seven years, the United States government granted the descendants of Sampson $466.66; however, her husband never got the chance to celebrate this, as he had died 11 months earlier.

The Committee on Revolutionary Pensions declared in 1837, "The whole history of the American Revolution records no case like this, and furnishes no other similar example of female heroism, fidelity, and courage… there cannot be a parallel case in all time."

In honor of her services and sacrifices, a statue was erected in her name outside the public library in Sharon. She was declared the official state Heroine of Massachusetts. To this day, Sampson is revered as one of the bravest female soldiers to join the United States Army. She was one of the first female symbols to present equality as a concept that could be achieved. Her story continues to inspire young women today to defy the barriers placed by society and attempt what is perceived by some as impossible and unthinkable.

Chapter 4: Dark Days of the Valley Forge: Stories of Pain and Hardship

Amid the American Revolutionary War, as 1777 gave way to winter, the Continental Army faced a daunting challenge. Fierce battles had been fought, resources were dwindling, and the army's morale was severely tested. To survive the harsh winter, they chose to establish their winter quarters in Valley Forge, Pennsylvania. However, this decision came at a heavy cost. Most soldiers were ill-equipped, lacking even the most basic necessities, such as shoes. The encampment was marked by overcrowded and rudimentary shelters and meager rations of flour and water. The situation was dire for both the soldiers and their horses, as many perished from starvation and exposure.

This bitter winter not only strained the resources of the Continental Army but also tested the resilience and determination of its soldiers. By the time spring finally brought relief, over two thousand soldiers had paid the ultimate price, succumbing to exposure and illness. In the face of such adversity, stories of courage, sacrifice, and leadership emerged from Valley Forge, showcasing the indomitable spirit of those who endured these trying times.

The Bitter Winter of Valley Forge

As winter set in, the Revolutionary War had already raged for two relentless years. Battles, including Lexington and Concord, Bunker Hill, Saratoga, and Trenton, had etched their place in history. However, by the end of 1777, the Continental Army, stationed at Whitemarsh, Pennsylvania, was ailing. General Sir William Howe's British forces had occupied Philadelphia, the American capital, dealing significant blows to the rebel cause. The army was demoralized, and supplies were dangerously low.

General Sir William Howe's British forces occupied the American capital.
https://commons.wikimedia.org/wiki/File:Gen._Sir_William_Howe.jpg

Amidst these challenges, General Washington made a pivotal decision. He established the winter encampment at Valley Forge, located approximately 20 miles from British-occupied Philadelphia. The decision was fraught with peril, but it carried strategic significance. Valley

Forge's proximity to Philadelphia was instrumental. It allowed Washington to monitor British movements, keep a watchful eye on the enemy's activities, and maintain the threat of a swift offensive.

Strategically, Valley Forge's natural defenses, with elevated terrain and the Schuylkill River, offered an advantageous position. It could serve as a strong deterrent to a British offensive. While Valley Forge offered no guarantee of ample supplies, the surrounding farmland held the potential to provide provisions, albeit intermittently.

As the Continental Army reached Valley Forge, they were confronted with a host of daunting challenges magnified by the unforgiving winter. Among the most glaring issues was the soldiers' dire lack of proper clothing. Many walked through the snow without shoes, leaving a trail of bloody footprints. Their frozen, injured feet were a stark testament to their sacrifice.

Shelter was another pressing concern. The soldiers, with little more than the rudimentary tools available, were tasked with constructing their own huts. These structures, often composed of logs, mud, and straw, provided limited protection against the biting cold and snow. The process of building these shelters was laborious and time-consuming, leaving the troops exposed to the unforgiving elements. Food shortages caused constant suffering. Soldiers subsisted on meager rations of small cakes made from flour and water, with infrequent access to meager portions of meat. Hunger became a relentless companion during this bitter winter.

The Continental Army's horses, which were essential for transportation and military operations, faced their own struggles. Starvation and exposure took a toll on these valuable assets, reducing the army's mobility. In the cramped and unsanitary living conditions of Valley Forge, deadly epidemics were rampant. Diseases like typhoid, dysentery, and smallpox claimed numerous lives and strained their limited medical resources.

Despite these seemingly insurmountable challenges, the soldiers at Valley Forge demonstrated unwavering determination and resilience. General Washington's leadership was paramount in maintaining morale and securing crucial supplies for the army. Additionally, the arrival of Baron von Steuben, a Prussian officer, marked a turning point. His expertise in military training and discipline transformed the Continental Army into a more professional and formidable fighting force.

Amid this bleak situation, General Washington exhibited remarkable leadership. He worked tirelessly to boost morale, maintaining discipline among his troops. He personally visited the suffering soldiers, sharing in their hardships and boosting their spirits. He also sought crucial supplies and support from Congress and nearby communities.

One story that stands out is that of Private Samuel, a young soldier from Maryland. He remained resilient despite losing several comrades to illness and seeing many others lose hope. He spent his free time helping his fellow soldiers build sturdier huts and shared what little food he had. His unwavering determination and positive attitude served as an inspiration to those around him.

Baron von Steuben's Training Revolution

As the relentless winter encased the camp in freezing temperatures and a blanket of snow, the soldiers huddled in makeshift huts... their spirits battered by a string of losses and their bodies weakened by malnutrition and sickness. The British held Philadelphia, and the revolutionary cause was teetering on the brink. But, as the soldiers huddled together, a glimmer of hope appeared on the horizon... an unexpected harbinger of change—Baron Friedrich Wilhelm von Steuben.

Baron von Steuben, a Prussian officer with an illustrious military background, arrived at Valley Forge with a fierce determination to change the course of the American Revolution. The Continental Army, though filled with patriotism and valor, was beset by disarray, and it lacked the professionalism needed to match the British regulars in combat. Recognizing this dire situation, Baron von Steuben embarked on a mission to instill discipline, order, and a sense of professionalism in the ragtag group of American soldiers.

His arrival couldn't have been more timely. As the soldiers braved the harsh winter, he wasted no time. With an authoritative presence, Baron von Steuben began to drill the troops tirelessly. His first lessons were fundamental—how to properly march, stand in formation, and handle their weapons. He demanded precision, discipline, and unwavering attention to detail.

The soldiers, who had endured the biting cold, sickness, and hunger at Valley Forge, initially met Baron von Steuben's rigorous demands with skepticism. However, as they began to witness the results of his training, their doubts slowly gave way to respect and admiration. They came to understand that these stringent methods were not meant to break their spirits but to mold them into a formidable fighting force.

One notable story that emerged during this transformative period was that of Sergeant Reynolds. Reynolds had been a seasoned soldier who had witnessed the Continental Army's trials and tribulations. His initial skepticism mirrored that of many others in the camp. However, Baron von Steuben's relentless training and his unyielding commitment to improving the soldiers' skills left an indelible mark on Reynolds.

Once disillusioned and weary, Sergeant Reynolds transformed into one of Baron von Steuben's most devoted pupils. His personal journey from a disheartened soldier to a disciplined and motivated leader became emblematic of the profound impact of Baron von Steuben's training.

The training regime was relentless, but the soldiers embraced it with newfound determination. They learned military tactics, the art of maneuvering on the battlefield, and the importance of teamwork. Discipline became the order of the day, and as the soldiers honed their skills, their confidence soared.

By the time spring arrived and the soldiers of Valley Forge emerged from their encampment, they were transformed. Baron von Steuben's relentless drilling and military expertise had redefined the Continental Army. Their improved morale, discipline, and newfound skills gave them a fighting chance in the battles that lay ahead.

As the Continental Army continued its campaign, the soldiers who had endured the bitter winter at Valley Forge, under the tutelage of Baron von Steuben, displayed remarkable resilience and professionalism on the battlefield. Their unwavering commitment to the cause of American independence was now matched by the military prowess they had acquired. Baron von Steuben's impact reverberated far beyond Valley Forge, as his methods and teachings would go on to significantly shape the Continental Army's future and contribute to the ultimate success of the American Revolution.

The Gift of Warmth

In the brutal winter of 1777-1778, as the Continental Army faced the merciless cold and heavy snowfall at Valley Forge, a heartwarming gesture of support emerged from the local communities. The soldiers were grappling with unimaginable hardships, their ranks lacking the proper clothing to withstand the relentless winter. The situation was dire, but the spirit of unity and sacrifice shone brightly.

Among the local residents, one individual from a long line of patriot ancestors felt a deep-seated obligation to make a difference. Inspired by the stories of their family's involvement in the Revolutionary War, they rallied friends, neighbors, and family members to join in their mission. On a particularly frigid night, this dedicated group assembled in a modest cottage. They brought any available yarn and materials, well aware that these seemingly ordinary resources could serve as a lifeline for the soldiers at Valley Forge. Their fingers worked tirelessly, weaving scarves, mittens, and socks... each stitching a token of support.

Weeks turned into months as the group continued their relentless efforts. Stories were shared about the soldiers' sacrifices, their unwavering commitment to the revolutionary cause, and the bitter winter they were enduring without proper clothing. As winter deepened, the tangible fruits of their labor took shape, which was a testament to their determination. With a wagon laden with their handcrafted goods, the volunteers embarked on a challenging journey to Valley Forge. The road was fraught with hardships, but their resolve never wavered.

Upon reaching the encampment, the volunteers were greeted with a moving sight. The soldiers, struggling to stay warm in their makeshift huts, welcomed the warm clothing with tearful eyes. The scarves, mittens, and socks were not merely physical items but also powerful symbols of the unwavering support of their fellow countrymen. The soldiers gratefully accepted the gifts, expressing heartfelt thanks for the solidarity of their fellow citizens. The act of kindness and the dedication of these volunteers provided not just warmth but also a profound sense of reassurance during the harshest days of winter.

The story of these dedicated volunteers and their community's unwavering support for the soldiers at Valley Forge is emblematic of the countless acts of kindness and solidarity that unfolded during the American Revolutionary War. It underscores the spirit of unity, the shared sacrifice, and the enduring commitment to the cause of American independence. The soldiers drew strength from knowing that they were not alone in their struggle and that the warmth of their countrymen's generosity could light up the darkest of winters.

Captain Benjamin Gilbert's Diary

Captain Benjamin Gilbert's diary provides a poignant and vivid firsthand account of the trials and tribulations faced by the soldiers at Valley Forge during the winter of 1777-1778. His entries offer a window into the daily struggles and unwavering determination of the Continental Army under the harshest of conditions.

In his diary, Captain Gilbert meticulously documented the devastating impact of the disease that swept through the encampment at Valley Forge. Soldiers fell ill to a variety of ailments, including smallpox, typhoid, and dysentery. The lack of proper sanitation, overcrowded living conditions, and exposure to the elements contributed to the rapid spread of these diseases. Gilbert's accounts provide specific details of the suffering endured by his fellow soldiers, illustrating the grim reality of their situation.

Captain Gilbert's writings paint a stark picture of the soldiers' inadequate clothing. Many of them lacked proper shoes, forcing them to resort to wrapping their feet in rags to protect themselves from the freezing conditions. The scarcity of warm clothing added to their misery as they struggled to stay warm through the bitter winter. Gilbert's diary entries offer specific instances of the soldiers' attempts to cope with these clothing shortages, showcasing their resourcefulness and determination.

Despite the harsh circumstances and widespread suffering, Captain Gilbert's diary also reflects the soldiers' unwavering spirit and resilience. His writings reveal their determination to persevere through adversity. The soldiers' sense of purpose and commitment to the revolutionary cause remained strong, even in the face of extreme hardship. This enduring spirit was a testament to their dedication to the American Revolution and their trust in their commander-in-chief, General George Washington.

Captain Gilbert's diary underscores the soldiers' deep trust in General Washington's leadership. He often wrote about how Washington's presence and personal commitment to their welfare served as a source of inspiration and motivation. Soldiers took solace in knowing that their commander-in-chief shared their hardships and was dedicated to securing the provisions and support they needed in order to endure the challenging winter. General Washington's unwavering determination was a beacon of hope that kept the soldiers moving forward.

Private Joseph Plumb Martin's Memoirs

Private Joseph Plumb Martin's memoirs offer a compelling and detailed account of the harsh realities faced by the soldiers at Valley Forge during the severe winter of 1777-1778. His writings provide a firsthand perspective on the brutal conditions endured by the Continental Army and their unwavering commitment to the revolutionary cause.

In his memoirs, Joseph Plumb Martin vividly depicts the dire shortage of shoes among the soldiers at Valley Forge. He describes how many soldiers, himself included, were forced to wrap their feet in rags due to the lack of proper footwear. Plumb Martin's accounts offer specific details of the soldiers' struggle to protect their feet, highlighting the extent of their physical suffering.

Despite the dire circumstances, Joseph Plumb Martin's writings reveal his unyielding dedication to the revolutionary cause. He maintained a steadfast commitment to the ideals of American independence, even in the face of adversity. His memoirs convey a deep sense of purpose and a strong belief in the importance of the revolutionary struggle. This commitment fueled his determination to endure the hardships of Valley Forge and to persevere through the darkest of times.

Throughout his memoirs, Joseph Plumb Martin's determination to endure the challenges of Valley Forge is evident. He did not waver in his resolve to continue the fight for American independence, even as the soldiers faced extreme suffering, hunger, and disease. Plumb Martin's writings illustrate the soldiers' remarkable resilience and their unwavering spirit, which enabled them to withstand the harsh winter and maintain their commitment to the revolutionary cause.

Amidst the chilling winter of 1777-1778 at Valley Forge, General George Washington's leadership and unwavering commitment to the Continental Army played a pivotal role in sustaining the soldiers through a challenging and dire period. Washington's actions, along with those of individual soldiers, showcased resilience, determination, and the indomitable spirit of the American Revolution.

George Washington's Leadership

General George Washington's leadership was marked by both strategic acumen and personal devotion to his troops. Valley Forge, approximately 20 miles from British-occupied Philadelphia, was chosen as the winter encampment due to its proximity to the enemy. This strategic decision allowed Washington to monitor British movements, maintaining a watchful eye on their activities while also posing a potential threat to the city.

Washington recognized the dire need for supplies, and he tirelessly worked to secure provisions for his troops. He wrote fervent letters to Congress, urging them to provide food, clothing, and equipment. His appeals and his dedication to the welfare of his soldiers were remarkable. Although the support was slow to arrive, his unyielding determination served as a source of inspiration.

Supplies finally began to arrive, and the soldiers' resilience in the face of adversity was a defining aspect of their experience. General Washington understood that boosting morale was crucial. He inspired his troops with his presence, often visiting the camp and engaging with his men. His enduring commitment to their welfare and unwavering determination were a source of strength.

As spring arrived, the soldiers emerged from Valley Forge. Their discipline, improved morale, and newly-acquired skills were instrumental in the battles that followed. The brutal winter had tested their mettle, but their remarkable resilience and determination ultimately contributed to the success of the American Revolution.

In essence, the winter at Valley Forge played a vital role in the American Revolution by forging a more resilient, disciplined, and determined Continental Army. The soldiers' unwavering commitment, the transformative leadership of General George Washington, and the resilience born out of adversity all contributed to the ultimate success of the revolutionary cause. Valley Forge remains an enduring symbol of the sacrifices made in the pursuit of American freedom and independence.

Chapter 5: The Battle of Saratoga: Turning the Tide of War

The Battle of Saratoga was a vital turning point in the Revolutionary War. The combination of the British surrender and the capability of the Americans built morale and was the bedrock on which American alliances with French forces were built. Two main battles were held in Saratoga, namely, the battle of Freeman's Farm and the battle of Bemis Heights. The foreign support provided by the French and the restored belief among Americans that they could win the war revitalized the spirit of the Continental army and other militias that joined them to fight.

The Battle of Saratoga was a turning point in the revolutionary war.
https://commons.wikimedia.org/wiki/File:Surrender_of_General_Burgoyne.jpg

The British approached Albany, New York, with three armies looking to converge in the center to overwhelm the American forces by flanking them on both sides. However, the British failed miserably against the superior military planning of American forces. In the aftermath of the battle, the British suffered almost 1,200 casualties, while the Americans only lost 330 of their soldiers. Impressed by the outcome of the battle, France signed the Treaty of Alliance with America, and later, the Dutch and Spanish offered help as well because they wanted to reduce Britain's monopolized power in Europe at the time.

Saratoga can be highlighted as the beginning and end of the empire's rule in the Americas. After this balance, independence no longer seemed like an unreachable goal, but it now became a tangible reality as the Americans grew in confidence. John Burgoyne was in charge of the attack that aimed to control the Hudson River Valley. However, Burgoyne returned to England disgraced, never holding a commanding position again. Vastly outnumbering the British at times and retreating strategically by knowing when to dispatch new units, the Americans were able to completely disseminate the British forces, which were low on supplies. The shifting tide of the battle shone a new light on America as an elite army that could not be underestimated. The foundation that was poured into Saratoga allowed the Americans to construct their tower toward ultimate victory.

Early Phases of the Northern Campaigns in the Revolutionary War

The war on the Northern Front lasted from 1775 to 1777. There were ups and downs in this period, with George Washington's army making critical mistakes against the well-executed maneuvers of the British navy. The resulting losses allowed the British to capture both Manhattan and Long Island. The Americans were close to defeat, but the British army held back, allowing them to regroup and re-strategize.

After independence was declared by thirteen colonies, separatist sentiments began growing and gaining popular support. One of the hubs of this revolutionary mindset was New England, where constant rebel agitation occurred. Therefore, the British devised a plan to keep New England isolated from the rest of the colonies in order to prevent the spread of separatist ideology among the southern regions, which the crown believed were more likely to be loyalists.

One of the major wins for Washington's forces was in Boston, where the general caused the British army to leave the area. Washington could not rest on his victory because he knew that the British would respond, so it was paramount for him to decide how they would proceed in the upcoming aftermath. Washington's concerns were valid because the British later took over New York, which was an amazing position to be controlled due to its geographical location being close to waterways, presenting a dividing buffer between strong separatist regions.

When the British drove Washington and his forces out of Manhattan, fighting continued at White Plains. Due to the losses suffered in Manhattan, Washington planned to penetrate Philadelphia, so the general settled in New Jersey. The British, under the control of William Howe, opted not to attack the Americans during this vulnerable point when they were low on supplies and motivation. George Washington saw the lack of aggression as an opportunity to attack both Princeton and Trenton. When the Continental Army had their backs against the wall, these miraculous victories renewed trust in Washington, and nobody would doubt his leadership skills.

Even after their devastating losses in New York, these initial victories captured the attention of leaders across Europe, who began respecting Washington's military prowess. The British still underestimated the American forces because, at this point, they were still comfortably winning the war with control of large, significant positions like New York and Canada. However, the Continental Army was still largely disorganized, with soldiers constantly deserting, along with other militias springing up that often derailed the Continental Army's plans. Washington found himself having to constantly correspond with Congress, pleading his case for a well-trained, professional army, as well as better logistical support to get supplies to areas that urgently needed them. Washington was fighting an uphill battle in the north prior to their decisive victories in Saratoga. At the end of 1776, the situation for the independence movement was looking bleak; however, some key miscommunications and incompetent execution of invasion plans in Saratoga allowed the war to turn around for the troubled Americans.

Initial Engagements of American Forces

The British plan was to come to New York from three different directions, converging in Albany. John Burgoyne marched down from Canada, defeating American troops in Vermont. Some of Burgoyne's troops were defeated in Bennington, resulting in him having a much smaller fighting force. Burgoyne reached the outskirts of Saratoga in September 1777. However, with his numbers already shrinking, he was ill-prepared to meet the soldiers under the command of General Horatio Gates. Gates commanded the Northern Department of the Continental Army and deployed 8,500 troops ready for the expected onslaught from Burgoyne. General Benedict Arnold and Colonel Daniel Morgan assisted Gates. Morgan commanded 500 skilled riflemen, which would come in handy against the British, who were better trained and organized.

The area, which was a dense forest, played in favor of Morgan's sharpshooting gunmen. By using nature to their advantage, the shooters were able to hide in the thick bush and ambush Burgoyne's men with constant rifle fire. Arnold and Morgan constructed forts and walls with heavy artillery and canons from which they could fire at enemies both on the road and in the river. The dense forest forced the British troops to use either the road or the river to attack, so they became easy pickings for the artillerymen.

Had Burgoyne had enough forces, and if he had coordinated with other British units, the outcome of this initial battle would have been different. Although Howe took a lot of the credit in letters, word quickly spread of the efforts of Benedict Arnold, who was hailed as a national hero among separatists across America before his unfortunate disgrace, which was based on political ambitions.

Huge American losses secured the strength of the British army before the tide of war turned. Before Burgoyne decided to march down from Canada to New York, the Americans had failed to invade the country that had strong allegiances to the crown. The three-pronged approach to converge on Albany failed dismally because of a lack of coordination, as well as no reinforcements or supplies being available to sustain the large army Burgoyne commanded.

The Battle of Saratoga Explained

The battle of Saratoga swung the war in favor of the American independence struggle. Before this point, America's forces seemed incapable of possibly coming out on top, with many soldiers leaving the battlefield after they encountered the overwhelming British might. The British, at the time, were both technologically and organizationally far ahead of where the Continental army was. However, through sheer perseverance, a little bit of luck, intelligence gathering, and strategic positioning, the Americans were able to manifest a pivotal win.

The British plan was for John Burgoyne to march down from Canada while Col. Barry St. Leger would approach Albany from Oswego by following the Mohawk Valley at the same time. The third component of the three-pronged approach was General Sir William Howe's army, which was coming up from the south toward the Hudson River. The goal of the plan was to leave the Americans overwhelmed by flanking them from all angles. The superior training and military arsenal of the British were meant to make easy pickings of the Americans in New York. The reason why they needed to control this area was to isolate New England, which was breeding rebellious sentiments. If the crown were able to stun the rise of the independence movement by keeping New England isolated, they would be able to convince their big base of loyalist support in the South to remain steadfast in supporting the empire.

As Burgoyne marched down to the Hudson River, there were many obstacles along the way. Burgoyne found forts that were abandoned by their commanders, who had probably been tipped off about his arrival. Burgoyne first reached Fort Ticonderoga, with his troops numbering 9000, including 3000 specialized German fighters. Battling through the unfavorable conditions of woods and swamps, Burgoyne reached the upper Hudson's Fort Edward, which was also evacuated by General Philip Schuyler, who retreated to the north of Albany in Stillwater. General Horatio Gates took over command of Schuyler's regiment. Burgoyne's men had suffered the long, strenuous journey, prompting him to send some of the German troops to Vermont so that they could plunder some horses and supplies. However, the German men were met with formidable forces under the command of General John Stark and Colonel Seth Warner. The fighters made light work of the Germans, completely eradicating the entire squad.

With his numbers dwindling and his army suffering from limited supplies, Burgoyne began worrying. His fear and anxieties were well-founded because St. Leger was having trouble at Fort Schuyler, being delayed more than he expected. The miserable cherry on the top for Burgoyne was finding out that Howe decided to abandon the mission, opting instead to head toward Pennsylvania. Burgoyne made the choice to keep pressing forward, bound by honor and his commitment to the fight. With only thirty days' worth of rations, the commander proceeded to cross the Hudson River and set up camp near Saratoga in New York. General Gates was overly prepared for Burgoyne's arrival, waiting for him in Bemis Heights with an unstoppable force of 12,000 men. Furthermore, Gates had access to reinforcements and supplies, which Burgoyne did not have the luxury of receiving.

The first battle of Saratoga on Freeman's Farm saw insanely high levels of British casualties as they were mowed down by Daniel Morgan's shooters, who utilized the woods for cover. The British marched through an open pathway, so they were easy pickings for the skilled marksmen who were accompanying Morgan. Once some British and German reinforcements arrived to support the disheartened forces of Burgoyne, they were able to recapture the open field, but they had already lost far more men than the Americans.

Howe was successful in capturing Philadelphia, but the victory ended up not meaning much in the broader context of the conflict. Henry Clinton, who ran the troops stationed in New York, captured forts on the Hudson but did not proceed toward Albany. Burgoyne waited patiently for the reinforcements that he thought they would get from Clinton, but they never arrived. Burgoyne was in a tough spot, so he made the executive decision to move without reinforcements... his pride did not allow him to retreat.

Burgoyne's slim numbers were not going to be enough to defeat the Americans in the second battle of Saratoga in Bemis Heights. Burgoyne had about 5,000 fight-ready men available, so he sent 1500 of them on a reconnaissance mission while the remainder of his army stayed behind. Continental infantry bravely fought off the British, and even though they outnumbered them, the British troops were more skilled and organized. However, as the American attack began dying down, Benedict Arnold came through as a saving grace, followed by a powerful brigade. With reinforcements from Gates and Arnold, the British were forced to flee. With his back against the wall, Burgoyne had no choice but to retreat. Gates had now assembled a team of 20,000 soldiers who surrounded the fleeing Burgoyne. This resulted in Burgoyne surrendering with his troops, who were all allowed to go back to Britain on the condition that they never set foot in America again. The marvelous military work of Gates put him in the running to replace George Washington, but this never came to fruition, as Washington remained the commander-in-chief until the British surrendered.

French Alliance Following the Battle of Saratoga

The seemingly impossible victory convinced France to support America's fight for independence. French and British relations were already shaky at the time, so they jumped at the opportunity to destabilize a part of the empire, which would serve to reduce Britain's influence in Europe. The French would now openly provide the Continental Army with military support. France considered England an enemy and would do anything to see their long-time rivals utterly disseminated, but they were not going to act if they felt it was a losing course. The French could not risk a British victory over them because of the tense relationship the two empires had.

The battle of Saratoga showed the French that there was a probability that America could win the war for independence. They now had renewed trust in the leadership of George Washington and could rest easy in the elite capabilities of the Continental Army. The French military alliance with the Americans provided them with wartime supplies like weaponry as well as personnel. Moreover, the French acted as diplomatic support for America in Europe. Without gaining help from the French, it would have been unlikely that the Patriots would have been able to stand firm against the immeasurable military might that the British Empire had behind it. The revolution not only needed popular support but also resource backing from global superpowers like France.

The French and American alliance was made official in 1778; however, the alliance started out shaky with the first French ship because troops were unable to dock at British-controlled harbors. This caused Charles d'Estaing, who commanded the fleet, to retreat to the Caribbean. However, the alliance began to strengthen, and the French proved crucial in ensuring American victory in the revolution. As much as France benefitted America, the same cannot be said for them. The war in America drained France financially, which caused a huge economic downturn in the country. Many theorize that the French Revolution in 1789 was a direct result of their involvement in the independence of America. The war in America quickly turned global as the Spanish and the Netherlands also got involved. Britain declared war on the Dutch, while France recruited their Spanish allies to assist in

America. The help that the French offered to America and abroad was central to winning American independence.

General Benedict Arnold

Although the history books remember General Benedict Arnold as a traitor, there was a time when numerous patriots sang his praises as a hero. His role in the independence of America was significant, and it should not be overlooked regardless of the actions he took later on. Arnold's success as a tactician in the battle of Saratoga may be why he ended up eventually betraying the revolution. The general rode in the frontlines, sustaining an injury to his legs. The troops that witnessed his bravery spread the length of his military skill, but in official documents and important circles, others took the credit for his success. Arnold's efforts went unrewarded, with many officers getting promoted while his rank did not increase. The hero had been placed on the back burner because others were allowed to claim credit that belonged to him by downplaying his bravery. This resentment is what guided Benedict Arnold's choice to betray his compatriots.

Benedict Arnold's life began spiraling as his wife participated in frivolous spending, which left the general in debt. He was eventually court-martialed for misconduct and financial impropriety. He beat both of the charges as he was exonerated, but Washington still viewed him in an unfavorable light. His resentment and desperation for money led him to conspire with the British by feeding them critical information about the ins and outs of the revolutionary movement. By the time Washington wanted him to rejoin the army in 1780, Arnold's bitterness had already consumed him. Arnold began sabotaging the Hudson River outpost while providing information to British Major John André by way of his wife. Arnold ended up leading troops against the Americans and also living in England with his wife, where he died in 1801. A large bounty was placed on his head, and any work he did to further the American cause was undone by his later actions; however, it is still undeniable that he played a pivotal role in shifting the war in the Patriots' favor.

Chapter 6: The Mohawk Valley: Tales of Betrayal and Loyalty on the Frontier

The essence of the American Revolution lay in the Mohawk Valley and its people. This region, which might seem minuscule in comparison to the size of the entirety of the USA, played a pivotal role in earning the freedom and independence of the nation. This chapter delves into the complexities of opposing interests and loyalties of the Mohawks and how each person's decisions, whether they were driven by fear, self-interest, or even morality, accompanied life-altering consequences.

Bridging between American colonies and British-governed Canada, the Mohawk Valley was among the most significant regions during the Revolutionary War. Its geographic location, which largely contributed to New York City's flourishing trade, exceptional agricultural activities, and economic growth, also made it a strategic and highly desirable location.

As conflicts escalated, the Mohawk Valley became home to a diverse population. Native tribes, European settlers, Patriots, and loyalists of British rule all lived and fought for their causes in this multifaceted terrain. After reading this chapter, you'll learn about the geographic and strategic features that distinguish the Mohawk Valley and understand the various factors that motivated its inhabitants to choose their allegiances. From economic and social ties to personal morals, beliefs, and interests, you'll uncover the driving forces that drove Americans to make critical decisions.

You'll also find out how Native American tribes in the Mohawk Valley became involved in the conflict and the far-reaching consequences of their entanglement in the Revolutionary War. Finally, you'll explore how families and friendships were torn apart in civil struggles and how the war finally came to an end, as well as gain insight into the lives of Patriots and loyalists following the nation's independence.

The Geographic Features of the Mohawk Valley

The Mohawk Valley area comprises 5,862 square miles, located in the northeastern region of the United States, mainly in New York. The valley is named after the Mohawk River, which flows through the Mohawk Valley into the Hudson River and eventually into the Atlantic Ocean. The river served as a navigational route for settlers, people, and goods, labeling the valley as a strategic and desirable location.

The region's lands were also very fertile, which heavily supported the agricultural industry, especially during the 18th and 19th centuries. Being a trade and agricultural hotspot, the Mohawk Valley and New York City as a whole experienced promising economic development. Interestingly, the Mohawk Valley is the only area in New York that does not share a border with another state – or with Canada!

The Historical Significance of the Region

The Mohawk Valley plays a significant role in the history of New York and the United States as a whole. Before the Europeans colonized the nation, the region was home to various Native tribes, including the Mohawk, Cayuga, Oneida, and Seneca. It was also the birthplace of the American Iroquois Confederacy. Native communities not only painted the region with valuable culture and history, but they also served as intermediaries, trade facilitators, and partners with European settlers. The first European settlers and explorers started building small towns in the area during the 17th century. The English colonizers followed their Dutch counterparts shortly after, giving rise to what is now known as New York City.

After colonizers approached the region with hopes of creating a "New World," this historical and cultural treasure became a war zone. To put it into perspective, one-third of all the Revolutionary Wars that took place in the United States were held in New York, half of which were fought in Mohawk Valley. The battle of Saratoga, one of the most significant struggles in American history, tipped the outcome in America's favor.

The Erie Canal: A Waterway to Economic Growth

The Erie Canal, one of the USA's most notable artificial waterways, was also constructed in the Mohawk Valley. This project allowed for the expansion of America's western frontier, enhanced commerce activities, and instigated the Industrial Revolution, in which the Mohawk Valley served as the center of operations. This ambitious project paved the way for more revolutionary undertakings, such as the establishment of the New York Central Railroad. The Erie Canal's intended function was to provide a cheap and safe transportation alternative to conduct trading activities.

While the project was proposed in 1768, it was not until 1808 that there was a general consensus among the relevant authorities that the Erie Canal would be a beneficial establishment. This led to the construction of the canal in 1817, garnering a lot of traffic and flourishing commerce activities only two years later, leading to the enlargement of the canal in 1836. Upon its completion in 1825, the 363-mile-long canal earned its title as one of the most incredible engineering innovations.

The canal was enlarged yet again in 1903 to catch up with the growing demand. It then incorporated three main branches: the Cayuga and Seneca Canal, the Oswego Canal, and the Champlain Canal. Serving as a link between the Hudson River and the Great Lakes, the Erie Canal further contributed to the region's economic growth.

American Citizens and Their Divided Loyalties

The fight for American freedom from British colonial rule was, in many ways, a civil war. Surprisingly, one-fifth of Americans were loyalists, meaning that they supported Britain during the uprising of the revolution. Loyalists' motivations to support the British government could be traced to self-interest or cowardice, according to the Patriots.

Loyalists and Why They Supported the British Crown

Many Americans, especially those who resided in the Mohawk Valley, had political, economic, and social ties to Britain. Many people were reliant on the trade and commerce activities that heavily relied on the settlers' goods and markets. The British government also offered grants to the settlers in the Mohawk Valley, among other parts of the USA, causing landowners to feel indebted to the British rule.

Many people felt afraid to speak up and rebel against the colonialist regime because they didn't want to risk losing their land titles. Many loyalists also had religious affiliations with the British Crown. The Anglicans, for instance, were historically devoted to the Church of England, causing members of this religious group to transfer their inherent loyalty to British rule.

People who had social or community-related connections to members of the British authority, such as military officials and other governmental personnel, might have felt loyal to these individuals, their positions, and their backgrounds. Many loyalists felt the obligation to respect these ties even if they didn't entirely agree with the British regime and policies.

The general consensus was loyalists were highly reluctant to join the fight for American freedom out of fear of reprisal. Everyone knew that the British crown was capable of inflicting harrowing consequences and persecution from local settlers if they had openly shown their support for the revolution. With that being said, Loyalists also faced a lot of hostility and pressure from non-loyalists. They fell victim to physical and verbal violence, exile, and property destruction as a consequence of supporting colonialism, which is why after the Revolutionary War came to an end, the British Parliament identified those who were in favor of the king's rule, offering them compensation for what they had endured.

Patriots and Their Motivations to Revolt

Patriots who openly displayed their desire for independence were driven by nationalistic ideals of liberty and democracy. Many inhabitants of the Mohawk Valley, along with others in the nation, strongly believed in the causes of self-advocacy, self-determination, and freedom. People were also more compelled to take a stand against the kingship because they were deeply affected by oppressive policies like the Quartering Act, which required colonial authorities to provide all sorts of amenities such as fuel, food and drinks, means of transportation, and quarters to the

British forces in their areas. Americans also had to pay taxes without getting anything in return for their money, and their incomes and economic growth were hindered by trade restrictions.

Many local leaders emerged to inspire patriots to advocate for their nation's freedom, allowing them to solidify their case and garner further support for the cause. Incursions and violent raids were often organized by the British army, causing Americans to feel the duty to protect themselves and their home. Patriots started establishing local military units and helped create a strong military in fear that they might be at risk of displacement and constant attacks. Those who lived in the Mohawk Valley went beyond protecting the area in which they lived. Many of them also enlisted in Continental or state militias and participated in regional campaigns targeted against British colonial rule and loyalists. They engaged in guerilla warfare tactics and set up defense units in an effort to destroy British supply lines and communications.

In addition to wanting to fight the injustices that resulted from British colonial rule, many patriots saw an economic and social opportunity in revolting. They knew that gaining their freedom would ultimately lead to economic growth and mobility since the trade restrictions would no longer be imposed. People would also live more freely and fairly without feeling terrorized and controlled.

No Room for Neutrality: The Pressure to Take Sides

Many of the citizens who took a neutral stance were forced to choose one of the two sides as the struggles escalated. The Patriots implemented a non-importation agreement that restricted the importation of goods and pledged loyalty oaths, causing many neutral individuals to join the stand against colonial powers. Others were harassed by loyalists and British militants to stand with colonialism.

Most people had to make choices that went against their personal morals and political views. For example, some religious groups, such as the Pennsylvania Quakers, who were against all forms of violence, had no choice but to stand with the loyalists because the Patriots highly demanded that all men of physical ability enlist in military service even if they desired to maintain a neutral stance. Some Patriot landlords also imposed high rents and wartime taxes on tenants, which caused many to believe that accepting British colonial rule would offer some economic relief.

People also made their decisions based on societal factors, such as ethnic prejudice. Scottish individuals who had recently moved to New England were subject to maltreatment by Americans, causing them to lean toward supporting British rule. Surprisingly, several Native American tribes felt that their land claims would be protected under the British kingship, causing them to turn to colonial powers for protection from American expansion. The British also found an opportunity to get more people enlisted in the British military and join the colonial cause by promising those who were enslaved by the Patriots freedom in exchange for their service.

The Rise of the American Revolution in the Mohawk Valley

In 1777, the British colonial powers ensued a multifaceted campaign in hopes of suppressing the American Revolution. Their main aim was to gain full control of the Mohawk and Hudson Rivers. This way, they'd be in charge of trade and economic activities while separating New England from other American colonies.

In pursuit of the campaign, the British forces embarked on various concurrent expeditions. They moved from Canada to the Southern American colonies while going eastward from Lake Ontario. The latter journey, however, was met with instant defeat. Other British forces were stationed in New York City. They believed that the decision to face General George Washington would be more beneficial than moving toward the northern colonies. Little did they know, however, that their stay in the Big Apple would be the main reason for their defeat, tipping the odds in the Patriots' favor.

Confronting the American General meant that the army would have little support when they faced unexpected resistance, which would lead to their defeat in Saratoga. This American win heightened the nationals' morale and encouraged France to ally with the United States against British powers, contributing to American independence.

The Battle of Oriskany

The Battle of Oriskany took place between British troops and revolting forces.
https://commons.wikimedia.org/wiki/File:Herkimer_at_oriskany.jpg

On the 6th of August, 1777, a battle between the British troops and the revolting forces of the Mohawk Valley broke out. British troops moved eastward toward New York and demanded that Fort Stanwix surrender to their powers. American militias, however, made their way to the besieged area from the Mohawk Valley to defend and free the territory. As the 800 Mohawks made their way toward Fort Stanwix, they were ambushed by 1200 British militiamen and some Iroquois allies near Oriskany Creek. This battle ended in many casualties on both sides. Despite what seemed like a promising outcome for the British forces, they were unable to capture Fort Stanwix. Although the battle ended with no clear winner, as both forces suffered significant losses, it was a clear setback for the British campaign.

Escalation Divisions

The pressure to take sides caused deep divisions between people, families, and friendships. This conflict extended to encompass Native American tribes as well. The groups were forced apart as they allied with conflicting forces. The upheaval also led to tragedies among European settlers. Around 24% of them were either murdered or had to flee the country. Around 33% of the remaining settlers relocated to Canada as loyalists. However, many of them eventually returned and engaged in ravaging activities against Americans. Settlers who didn't go anywhere had to defend their properties and help support George Washington's army.

The status quo only got worse after the Americans' win in the Battle of Oriskany and the British defeat at Saratoga. Wanting to salvage what was left of their power, the British power started attacking defenseless inhabitants of the Mohawk Valley. This tragic incident is now known as the "Burning of the Valleys." In retaliation, the Patriots started the "Border Raids" as a form of revenge. This period of back-and-forth violence was tough for both sides – militants and innocent civilians alike. Members of the same communities and tribes were pitted against each other, and these struggles impacted all aspects of the lives of everyone involved until the end of the Revolutionary War.

Newfound Hope

1781 was a turning point in the lives of the Mohawks. Hopes, dreams, and redemption emerged from what felt like endless suffering, injustices, and defeat. This newfound positivity was all attributed to Colonel Marinus Willet, who was appointed by General George Washington to be in charge of the Mohawk forces. The new Colonel in command led the frontier through a series of victories. He also revived the agricultural industry in the region. Under the colonial powers, the fertile grasslands and farms were destroyed by raids. Crops and resources were burned, plummeting the region's economic growth and the ability to sustain itself. Willet, however, helped restore the lands to their initial conditions. Under his leadership, the fields became abundant with wheat and other sustenance crops.

Not only did an abundance of produce reassure people that they would have enough to eat, but it also instilled their hopes for a better future. Fear and their sense of uncertainty and insecurity had now started to dissipate. People who fled in terror started returning to their homelands, and families, friendships, and social connections were being restored. In 1783, General George Washington thought it only right to visit the Mohawk Valley to thank and honor those who made unparalleled sacrifices in pursuit of American independence.

What Happened to the Loyalists?

The British defeat and the freedom of America meant that loyalists would never be able to return to their homeland. How could they face the people who fought, experienced insurmountable losses, and gave up so much to earn their nation's freedom? Around 7500 of the whopping

60,000 to 80,000 Americans who left the nation settled in Great Britain. Other loyalists tried to make Canada, Spanish Florida, or the Caribbean their homes, while the minority attempted to return to the United States.

Wherever they settled, most of the loyalists didn't feel at home. They either struggled with poverty or felt extremely homesick. Black loyalists, however, had it worst of all. They either caught life-threatening diseases, suffered from acute poverty, or were recaptured as enslaved people and sold in the Caribbean. Even after suffering the mortifying consequences of supporting the enemy, many loyalists still felt uncertain about America's future as a free nation. Others, however, naturally regretted their choices and wished they had fought for their nation's freedom.

The Mohawk Valley's historical significance is associated with its geographical and strategic location, along with its function as a tapestry of various cultures, opposing forces, and allegiances. This region played a pivotal role in the establishment of British colonial powers, the rise of the Revolutionary War, and the independence of the United States, earning it its title: "the Gateway to the West."

This title serves as a symbol of the region's role in transportation and trade and signals its role as a gateway to new hopes, beginnings, and opportunities. The Mohawk Valley witnessed pivotal moments in United States history, and it serves as an enduring testament to the willpower and determination of its residents.

Chapter 7: The Traitor's Treason: Stories Surrounding Benedict Arnold's Betrayal

Whether you are familiar with American history or not, you have probably heard the name Benedict Arnold before. In fact, the name has become synonymous with the word "traitor." Arnold was an American hero who turned his back on his country and became one of the biggest traitors in history. This chapter tells the story of the rise and fall of Benedict Arnold.

History books remember General Benedict Arnold as a traitor.
https://commons.wikimedia.org/wiki/File:Benedict_Arnold_1color.jpg

Benedict Arnold's Early Life

Arnold was born on January 14, 1741, in Norwich, Connecticut. He was the son of Hannah Arnold and Benedict Arnold III, a prosperous businessman. His mother was an affluent widow who had received a substantial amount of money from her previous spouse. Arnold and his siblings attended private schools due to their affluent parents' support. He has three sisters and two brothers. Sadly, yellow fever claimed the lives of two of his sisters and all of his brothers when they were quite small. Their father became depressed and started drinking as a result, and the family lost everything. Arnold had to drop out of private school, as did his sister Hannah.

Arnold's life took an unexpected turn. His parents were careless, and he had no structure after school. That's why he was in trouble all the time. His mother put him to work at her cousin's apothecary because she was upset about her son's unruly behavior. Arnold enlisted in the militia at the age of sixteen and participated in the French and Indian War. Arnold got into the service, but he continued to work with his cousins.

In 1759, his mother passed away from yellow fever, and he became the caretaker of his father and sister. His father was devastated by his wife's death, and his drinking got worse until he died in 1761. Arnold then left his work with his cousins and decided to open his own apothecary with his sister, Hannah. However, his business dealings turned to smuggling, which was against British laws. He grew frustrated with the Crown's taxes and restrictions. In 1766, he joined the Sons of Liberty, a secret group opposed to the British taxing laws.

In 1767, Arnold married Margaret Mansfield, and they had three sons. The couple settled in New Haven.

Benedict Arnold's Early Military Career

Before Arnold betrayed his country, he was a war hero and led many battles against the British.

Siege of Fort Ticonderoga

Arnold rose to the rank of Captain in the Governor's Second Company of Guards before the Revolutionary War. Upon learning of the Battles of Lexington and Concord, he was eager to lead his soldiers on a mission to seize Fort Ticonderoga. He requested authorization from the Committee for Safety, and they allowed it. However, Ethan Allen, an American soldier, and his group, known as the "Green Mountain Boys," joined Arnold's militia since they shared the same objective. Since Arnold couldn't rely on this gang and they were unpredictable, he wasn't happy to see them. He went to Ft. Ticonderoga with both leaders and their soldiers after attempting to persuade Allen of his point of view but failing.

They surprised the British and managed to capture the fort without spilling one drop of blood. This was the Continental Army's first victory, which gave them hope and boosted their morale. Ironically, Arnold won this battle with the help of a British spy.

The Green Mountain Boys celebrated their victory by getting intoxicated. They also didn't respect Arnold or follow his commands. He was very angry with their behavior, and he often clashed with Allen. Both men couldn't have been more different, and they rarely saw eye to eye. However, they only agreed on one thing... invading Canada.

In 1775, Arnold lost his wife, Margaret, while he was still at Ft. Ticonderoga.

Battle of Quebec

Arnold and his men headed to Quebec. Since he didn't have the resources to attack the city, he first asked them to surrender peacefully, but his request was denied. He had no choice but to wait for assistance. General Richard Montgomery brought troops and supplies and joined Arnold. Again, they demanded for the city to surrender. However, Quebec governor Guy Carleton knew the Americans would never be able to destroy his fort and capture their city. He was right.

Arnold and Montgomery attacked the city with their men. However, the British were prepared for them and fired at them from the city's walls. Sadly, Montgomery was killed right away, and his men had no choice but to retreat. Arnold and his men were also under attack. Many were killed, and he suffered from a serious leg injury. Unfortunately, the Battle of Quebec was a disaster and a military failure. Hundreds of soldiers were captured, wounded, or killed at the hands of the British.

The Battle of Ridgefield

After his leg healed, Arnold was ready to go back to battle. In 1777, he and his men faced the British in Connecticut. William Tryon, the British governor of New York, received information about a Continental Army weapons depot. Tryon and his men succeeded in capturing the weapons and causing serious damage to the American army. Although the British won this battle, they suffered more casualties than the Americans. Arnold was a brave and strong soldier. He managed to escape from the British after they shot two of his horses, and he returned home safely.

Arnold achieved many military successes over the years. He captured Fort Ticonderoga, showed immense bravery during the Battle of Quebec, and was considered a Patriot hero. However, he didn't feel that he received any recognition for his hard work. In 1777, five officers were promoted above him. Arnold felt insulted and quit the army. However, General George Washington was convinced to reconsider his decision.

Battle of Bemis Heights

Arnold listened to Washington's advice and rejoined the Continental Army. During the fall of 1777, Arnold defended New York from a British invasion. He served under General Horatio Gates. However, both men couldn't stand each other. This drove Gates to relieve Arnold from his command.

In the Battle of Bemis Heights, Arnold defied Gates, took a group of soldiers, and attacked the British army. This caused confusion among the enemy lines, which was a key factor in America's victory. If it wasn't for Arnold, the Americans wouldn't have won the battle. He deserved recognition and a promotion for his role. However, Gates took all the credit for himself and didn't mention Arnold's heroism in his reports.

Battle of Saratoga

Arnold's biggest military achievement took place in the Battle of Saratoga. He showed exemplary leadership and bravery. Under his command, his men achieved a great victory against the British army. Thousands of enemy soldiers ended up surrendering to Arnold – a big humiliation for the Crown. This battle changed the course of the war, resulting in an alliance between America and France.

Arnold injured his leg again. His wound was so serious that he wouldn't be able to go back to the field for a while. General Washington made him Philadelphia's military governor until he recovered. However, Arnold's feelings toward his country started to change.

The Fall of a Hero

How could a hero who loved his country and was willing to die for it suddenly change his loyalty? Arnold was always passed over for promotions and recognition, and he never felt appreciated by the country to which he gave his heart and soul. He became angry and sold out everything he ever held dear.

Disputes with Officers

Gates wasn't the only person to downplay Arnold's achievements in the war. Eason also diminished his role in the Battle of Fort Ticonderoga, and the two constantly fought and disagreed with each other.

Although he brought his country close to independence, he often felt overlooked, leading to many fights with his superior officers. He had more enemies than friends for constantly pointing out that he never got any recognition. He fought with James Easton, militant soldier Josh Brown, and General Moses Hazen.

Even his fellow officers didn't appreciate his behavior. They found him greedy, emotional, and vain. One officer even said that Arnold worshiped money and would do anything to be rich - even sell out his own country. Clearly, some people predicted Arnold's turning to the dark side.

His Second Injury

Arnold was very frustrated to be injured in the same leg again. He spent four months recovering at a hospital. During this time, he thought about the unfair treatment he received from his superiors and how many times they promoted others over him. He sacrificed so much for his country that he paid from his pocket to support the American troops. He gave up his apothecary business so he could fight for America's independence, and this was the thanks he got.

After he returned to the army, congress only restored his rank without his seniority. Arnold was livid for facing injustice once more. However, Washington later restored his seniority... a gesture that wasn't welcomed. He wrote Arnold a letter to deliver the good news; however, Arnold didn't write back right away. He was disappointed that Congress had recognized Gates as the hero of Saratoga and given him a medal when it was Arnold who had led them to victory. When he sent a letter to Washington, he used the words "your country," referring to America. This was two and a half years before his betrayal. However, it was clear that he was distancing himself from his country and the war as he no longer felt any kind of connection or patriotism.

Court-Martial

During his time in Philadelphia, Arnold married Peggy Shippen, and they had five children together. However, this wasn't entirely a marriage based on love and romance. Peggy was 20 years younger than him, and her father was a Loyalist sympathizer and held high status in the city. Marrying Peggy brought Arnold the social status he had always wanted. However, her father wasn't a wealthy man, so Arnold had to find another way to live the life of his dreams.

He put himself in huge debt so he and his wife could live a lavish lifestyle. His spending raised some eyebrows, and many wondered how he got the money. This led to the interference of the Continental Congress. They accused him of 13 misconducts. A court-martial was convened, and Arnold heard the accusation against him that included illegal trade and misusing government wagons.

Arnold was hurt listening to the unjust charges. After years of serving his country with honor and a clean record, he found himself in a military court, having to defend himself against crimes he didn't commit. Things got worse for him when he asked Congress for support during his trial, and they refused.

Military officer and lawyer Joseph Reed was asking for delays throughout the trial mainly to collect evidence, but he also wanted to torture Arnold. Washington didn't try to stop the delays. Reed threatened him that if he interfered, he wouldn't get the support of the Pennsylvania militia. Washington secretly wanted to help Arnold, but he needed the troop-support more.

The trial was interrupted by a British attack. Arnold was tried and acquitted of most of the charges a few months later. However, the court commanded General Washington to publicly reprimand him.

This injustice increased his anger toward his country. He spent months listening to Reed make false claims and ruining his good name, and then he was betrayed by Congress and Washington. He saw everyone as an enemy, even Washington. From the moment he was reprimanded, Arnold was bitter and believed his patriotism had ruined his life.

Washington wanted to make peace with Arnold, so he offered him command of a wing of the Continental Army, but he refused and demanded West Point instead. Washington agreed. Little did he know of what Arnold had in mind.

Peggy

Peggy had a few British connections, which she used to push her husband to switch sides. She was a good friend of British Major John André, and she introduced him to Arnold. Peggy grew accustomed to a certain lifestyle that her husband wasn't able to fulfill. The only way she could live the life she desired was if her husband joined the British.

Both men began corresponding with one another. Arnold was no longer a loyal soldier but a traitor to himself and his country.

Treason

Arnold chose to command West Point for a reason. This place held strategic value in controlling lines of transportation and communication between New England and all the other states. He was in possession of very sensitive information. In his correspondence with André, he revealed to him locations of supply depots, troop locations, defensive positions, planned movements, and troop strengths.

They would often use Peggy as an intermediary as no one would suspect her. The letters were also coded and written in invisible ink.

Of course, this information wasn't free. Arnold took 10,000 pounds from the British to switch sides.

West Point

In 1779, Arnold reached out to General Henry Clinton and explained his desire to pledge allegiance to the British. He was sending Clinton sensitive information through André. However, Clinton had his eyes on West Point for its significant strategic position. Arnold provided the British with the perfect opportunity to capture the fort without going into battle. Clinton offered Arnold 20,000 pounds to deliver 3,000 troops to West Point. Since Arnold was in debt and blinded by his greed, he agreed to his offer.

He even offered the British to deliver General Washington to them for free. However, his plan didn't work, as Washington had already escaped by the time Lincoln received his letter.

Arnold used his critical position to weaken the West Point defense line. He drained its supplies and refused to order any repairs. However, he told Washington that it could withstand any attack.

Arnold was driven by vengeance and was willing to do whatever it took to punish the people he once called his comrades. He believed people like Gates and Allen should pay for taking credit for his work and ruining his reputation.

John André's Capture

In 1780, André and Arnold met to discuss the strategy for surrendering West Point. However, their plan failed as André was captured a few days later. The Americans found Arnold's letters with André, thus exposing his betrayal. When Arnold learned about André's capture, he took his wife and kids and fled to Britain while André was executed.

Arnold fought his people alongside the British. One would think he would hide away after his betrayal was discovered; however, he continued his despicable acts. He attacked his home state, Connecticut, and tried to capture Thomas Jefferson.

For centuries, historians tried to figure out Arnold's motives. At first, one could say that his greed, anger, and unjust treatment drove him to vengeance. However, there was no excuse for fighting against the men who, just a year ago, were your soldiers and under your command.

Although Arnold sold out his country for the British, they never really trusted him. In fact, many found him dishonorable and immoral. A man who sold his country for money would betray anyone. They treated him as a tool to fulfill their goals. They even gave him 6,000 pounds instead of the 20,000 they promised. He was also prohibited from holding any position in the army.

After the Revolutionary War, Arnold lived in London. However, the English people were very cold toward him as they blamed him for the death of André, whom they considered a hero. When he and his wife attended a public gathering, people would hiss at them. The English press regularly criticized him and his wife.

He then left for Canada, where he worked as a merchant, but he wasn't welcomed there as well, so he returned to London. He was accused of spying and spent a few years in prison during the French Revolution.

He died at the age of 60 and was denied military honors at his burial.

George Washington

Understandably, Washington was hurt, angry, and disappointed when he discovered Arnold's betrayal. It might not seem like it to Arnold, but Washington tried to protect him as best as he could.

Washington ordered Major Henry Lee to capture Arnold. Lee sent Sergeant John Champe, who pretended to join the British forces, to find and abduct Arnold. However, Arnold was transferred at the last minute, ruining the plan.

If Arnold could go back in time, do you think he would have made the same choices? Since Arnold was a traitor, most people regard his character as evil. However, people's actions shouldn't be judged as either black or white. One could see him as a victim of circumstances that were beyond his control, while others might say that Arnold shouldn't have asked for anything in return for serving his country.

Many people still ask if Arnold was a victim or a traitor. However, there is never any excuse for betraying one's country and killing the people who once fought by your side.

It's all these levels and complexities that make Benedict Arnold's story one of the most interesting tales in American history.

Chapter 8: The Battle of Cowpens: Daniel Morgan's Tactical Genius

For two long years, after the conflict arose in the towns of Concord and Lexington on April 19, 1795, sparking the American Revolution, the battles were mostly limited to the northern fields. During the second year, the British suffered a loss at the Battles of Saratoga in September and October 1977, and the French entered the scene on the American side. In an attempt to reverse their fortunes, the British launched their campaign on the Southern fields, marking the foundation of what became known as the Southern Theater of the Revolutionary War. While participating in many battles throughout the final years of the war, the South became a pivotal theater, giving rise to the battles of Yorktown, Camden, Guilford Courthouse, and Cowpens. Besides outlining the strategic importance of the Southern Theater in the Revolutionary War and the shifting dynamics of the conflict, this chapter will also introduce key figures involved in the Southern Theater, including British commander Banastre Tarleton and American commander Daniel Morgan. The next section will provide insight into the life of Daniel Morgan and his contributions to the American cause. The following sections will discuss the strategic movements and decisions that led to the confrontation at Cowpens and the key battles in which Daniel Morgan was involved.

Daniel Morgan contributed a lot to the American cause.
https://commons.wikimedia.org/wiki/File:DanielMorgan.jpeg

The Southern Theater

Even though tempers in the South flared as far back as April 20, 1775 (immediately after the battle of Lexington and Concord on the North) when the British recaptured gunpowder storage at Williamsburg, this was only one of the small skirmishes that marked the fight on the South. On November 17, 1775, the British clashed with the Patriots at the Battle of Kemp's Landing in Virginia, which was the Brits' attempt to conquer a deep-water port they needed in order to begin their southern battle campaign.

Beyond tactical advantage, the British were motivated by another possible gain. Unlike the New England Colonies, which produced the same gains as the British Isles, the plantations in the South yielded much more. Here, tobacco, indigo, rice, and other crops grew, promising a much bigger economic gain as these didn't grow in Britain. At the same time, the slavery practices kept the prices of this product low, so the British saw it as a win-win situation.

In June 1776, the Brits made their first major attack, led by Commodore Sir Peter Parker and British Major General Sir Henry Clinton. Their attempt to take over Charleston was unsuccessful as they failed to conquer Fort Sullivan (the city's main defense line) and were defeated by Commander Moultrie.

Despite this and several other defeats, the British Loyalist support slowly grew in the south, providing an ample supply of Loyalist civilians and enslaved people from patriot plantations who would take the place of redeployed soldiers needed in foreign wars. After finding so many allies to support their cause, the Brits devised the Southern Strategy, which recast the American Revolution into a far more personal cause. In the Southern Theater, it wasn't uncommon to find brothers fighting against brothers, each campaigning for their own cause.

After finally conquering Savannah in December 1778, the British finally gained a strategic foothold in the South. A year and a half later, the Henry Clinton-led campaign conquered another key port, this time in Charleston. In mid-1779, Clinton declared that slaves who escaped their masters would be granted freedom and shelter. Although they wouldn't be required to fight on the British Loyalist side, they were welcomed to remain as nurses, cooks, and any position they could find. This was one of the crucial moves in the Southern Theater, as it bolstered the Loyalists' ranks while delivering a major blow to the Patriots' economy.

To further entice conflicts in the South, the British Loyalist leaders often resorted to strategies like fearmongering and pillaging patriot plantations. One of these leaders was Colonel Banastre Tarleton, who, after engaging mixed-race parties to attack and cause fears of a social revolution, even went as far as killing patriots wanting to surrender after the Battle of Waxhaws in 1780.

Unfortunately, the continued threats and intimidation techniques they used against the enslaved population backfired on the Brits. Instead of gaining more allies, they alienated the majority of the population, who were less than sympathetic to their cause. The fact that they aggravated a civil war within a civil war didn't help either. Losing support just as fast as they had gained it previously, the Loyalists faced seemingly insurmountable challenges in battle as they continued their campaign in the Southern Theater.

At the same time, after Charleston's fall, the Patriot's defense relied entirely on frontier and rebel troops. These were led by former plantation owners, whose property was destroyed by Tarleton's men and surviving commanders. Taking a page from the tactical guide, their frontiers employed to conquer the Native Americans, and the rebels engaged in surprise nighttime raids against trains and outposts, decimating British supplies.

Meanwhile, the Loyalist British troops engaged in even more devastating attacks, refusing to spare people, livestock, or homes. In retaliation to their massacres, the Patriots started to kill Loyalists, often waving flags while doing so. This led to numerous confrontations between the two sides, including the one at King's Mountain on October 7, 1780, where the Loyalist military party was defeated by a Patriot troop twice its size.

Wanting to bolster their cause, in December 1780, the Americans placed one of their most prized assets - Commander Nathanael Greene - on the front of the Southern Theaters' Continental Army. Around the same time, Cornwallis, the leader of a party under Commander Tarleton, launched an even greater siege on the Patriot activities in both North and South Carolina. To counter this move, Nathanael Greene sent a troop led by a man who he knew could rise to the occasion and stop Tarleton's party in its tracks... Daniel Morgan.

Daniel Morgan, the American's Most Valuable Asset

While little is known about Daniel Morgan's early childhood, he was likely born in 1735. As a child of Welsh immigrants in New Jersey, Morgan showed a rebellious streak from an early age, finally leaving home in 1752. Initially heading west, Morgan's journey took him to Winchester, Virginia, where he settled and started working as a wagoner. His profession made him an excellent recruiter for the British Army in the wake of the Indian and French War. Heading the teams hauling freight to the colony's eastern part, Morgan made a significant contribution to supplying the British Army. However, he made the mistake of accompanying General Edward Braddock during his attempt to overthrow the French and Indians at Fort Duquesne. After being struck by a soldier with a sword, Morgan retaliated by knocking the man over. He was punished with a staggering 500 lashes. Morgan survived the otherwise fatal punishment, bearing the deep scars until his death and joking that the punishing officer miscounted and he was only given 499 lashes instead of the full 500. Later on, he suffered another near-fatal injury when he was shot in the back of his neck by Indians who ambushed the company of rangers he allied himself with in the Shenandoah Valley.

After another miraculous recovery, in 1774, Morgan took to farming, working alongside the captain of the Frederick County Militia. Shortly after the American Revolution began, he chose to support the Patriots by leading a group of riflemen to the siege of Boston in 1775. Fueled by his disdain for the British Loyalists, Morgan trained his group to become seasoned fighters and tacticians. Soon, they became known as "Morgan's riflemen" and were praised for their incredible accuracy. They wore hunting shirts, distinguished themselves from other groups, and struck fear in the British anywhere they appeared. Due to the imminent fear factor, the garment became the uniform of the Continental Army.

In 1775, he was appointed leader of a Virginia rifle company destined to support the campaign for the invasion of Canada. While originally assigned to watching the company, Morgan was forced to take over the campaign when both his superiors, Colonel Benedict Arnold and General Richard Montgomery, fell at the battle of Quebec. Despite his best efforts, Morgan's company was too small to withstand the counterattack, and once again, he found himself at the mercy of the British forces. Months later, he was released and promoted to colonel of a Virginia regiment. Here, he added even more to the growing list of skills he developed after serving in the British army and as the leader of the Virginia riflemen.

One could say that Daniel Morgan was a man ahead of his time. He employed tactics that went far beyond what was considered standard warfare at the time. Soon after he was appointed a colonel, he was leading an infantry corps, instructing the men to disturb the highly-disciplined British troops. Disguising themselves as Indians, Morgan's group made several blitz attacks on the British in New Jersey and New York in 1797. Later in the same year, under the orders of George Washington, Morgan joined General Horatio Gates' army, which took him to the Battle of Saratoga. Morgan proved to be an instrumental asset in the battle, given that one of his highly-trained riflemen took down British General Simon Frase, helping the Americans gain the upper hand. While this led to the surrender of the British General, John Burgoyne, at Saratoga, General Gates even admitted that Colonel Morgan's group was the most fearsome part of the corps, highly praising the men, but Morgan was passed over for a promotion. After being appointed as colonel of a different Virginia Regiment, he mounted even more victories, but his leaders refused to promote him. After being thoroughly disillusioned when he wasn't given brigadier general and command of a new rifle corps that he wanted in 1779, Morgan resigned from the army.

However, after suffering several devastating losses under Gates's commands, including the one at the Battle of Camden in South Carolina, to General Lord Charles Cornwallis, the Americans were desperate for Morgan's expertise. Still nursing his wounded pride, Morgan initially refused to join, but he soon relented and rejoined Gates in the Southern Theater. After arriving in North Carolina in 1780, Morgan took over an independent corps, supporting state militia. However, after reconsidering the results of the Battle of Camden, Georgia, Washington decided to appoint a new general in the South: Nathanael Greene. Subsequently, Congress also promoted Morgan to brigadier general under Greene's command. Deciding on a new tactic against the British army, Greene split his troops, deploying Morgan to South Carolina. The advantage they gained was twofold. They found it easier to feed smaller groups while the British were forced to confront the American troops on two separate fronts. Upon their arrival in January 1791, Morgan learned that Colonel Banastre Tarleton's group, led by Charles Cornwallis, was preparing to attack his army. The first attack happened days after at Cowpens.

The Battle of Cowpens

Greene's tactic to employ smaller groups at a time soon paid off. When Cornwallis learned that Daniel Morgan arrived at the British back front with only 700 members of the militia and 300 riflemen, he immediately sent a group of 1,100 Loyalists and Redcoats to counter Morgan's moves. The group was led by Banastre Tarleton, who, encouraged by the Camden victory and other triumphs, found it a much-welcome challenge to aggressively pursue Morgan's troops through South Carolina. While considering Morgan's groups too small to do much damage to the British army, Cornwallis also knew of Morgan's fame as a cunning strategist and tactical genius. He feared Morgan would try to ignite a Patriot uprising in the South in order to bolster the numbers of his group, yet confident in his men's ability to emerge victorious again, Cornwallis proceeded to attack. Morgan, on the other hand, backed up his men all the way to the river of Cowpens, seemingly intent on meeting Tarleton there despite being in a vulnerable position. After all, once the British crossed the Pacolet River, the Americans found themselves between them and an open pasture land (and the Broad River) that offered little cover for Morgan's famous riflemen. However, the British troops consisted mostly of cavalry, who found it easy to maneuver the terrain. What the Brits failed to realize was that their enemy found a sloping bridge dipping down and rising again, providing shallow and higher points at the same time for the riflemen. Knowing the area well, Morgan also found another bridge that could hide his cavalry, which could wait in ambush. Having surveyed the terrain and identified the tactical points he could use to his advantage, Morgan set on to devise a winning strategy against Tarleton's army.

However, Cornwallis had good reason to fear him because Morgan had a few tricks up his sleeves. Fearing his men would panic at the sight of the ranks of a much more organized British army (which is what led to the Camden defeat months before), Morgan set on to boost their morale by ensuring they'd be safe between the two rivers. He also counted on the Brits' well-versed tactic of lining up the troops for a strict linear assault, which is exactly what Cornwallis did. Meanwhile, Morgan left his lines a little more open, as if extending an invitation for attack.

Moreover, his plan further divided his group and used the cavalry, militia, and civil fighters at different tactical points. As Tarleton was preparing to attack, Morgan immediately deployed a line of skirmishers who were backed up by a militia line. This was a form of ruse as the skirmishers were to fall back after the militia as soon as they fired two rounds. Led by Colonel Andrew Pickens, the militia briefly left the battlefield with the skirmishers in tow. This confused the British, who thought that both lines were retreating while degenerating into a rout. However, behind the militia, the Continental regulars and Lieutenant Colonel William Washington's cavalry were waiting for the unsuspecting Brits, who ran into tactical-deployed rifle fire and attack from the cavalry at the same time. Even worse, according to a previously-established plan by Morgan, the militia line was reformed behind the Continental Regulars line, reinforcing the magnitude of their attack.

Twenty-five miles west of Kings Mountain, Tarleton's troops split their lines to attack the Americans. Immediately afterward, Pickens reformed the militia on their left while Washington took the cavalry to their right. Flanked on both sides, the British troops never stood a chance. Although Tarleton escaped unscathed, he made the choice to retreat too late to save any of the 702 captured or 110 killed by the Americans. Decimating the British army so severely helped Daniel Morgan enter the history books as a hero of the American Revolution. While he previously participated in many battles and led numerous successful rifle corps to battle, none of his groups were as triumphant as the ones that earned the victory of Cowpens.

Meanwhile, the Americans suffered fewer than 100 casualties, scoring the first and most successful Patriot victory in American history. What made this triumph even more outstanding was the battlefield itself, where Morgan's troops were considered to be at a disadvantage both based on their current geographical location and the surprise attack the British were about to launch on them. They only had Morgan's vast strategic experience to assist them, and this was proven to be enough.

Genius tactics and victory aside, this wasn't the American's only clash with Cornwallis. Furious for having lost a major chunk of his army on January 17 (some say he even broke his saber when he heard the number of casualties), Cornwallis retreated from the North and South Carolina border but soon reformed his troops and was ready to attack again. While empowered by his sound success, Green's troops didn't have the same luck the next time they met Cornwallis' lines. This took place at the Battle of Guilford Courthouse on March 15, 1781, in North Carolina, where Greene was forced to retreat in defeat. Still, despite having to lose to the British, the Americans suffered far fewer casualties. This time, Cornwallis lost a third of his army, which caused quite an uproar in the British parliament, with some claiming that another victory like that would be detrimental to the entire British army.

Combined with the victory at the battle of Cowpens, despite the defeat, the lack of casualties provided an important morale boost to the Americans. Later in the same year, they emerged victorious once again at the last major Revolutionary War battle at Yorktown, Virginia. Both Morgan's trump at Cowpens and Cornwallis's latter losses debilitated his army, facilitating General Washington's easy victory in Yorktown. However, despite his best efforts and Washington's wishes, Morgan himself wasn't able to participate in his battle.

Suffering from chronic sciatica (nerve inflammation in the back) since his battle of Quebec a decade and a half earlier, Morgan found it very painful to ride a horse. His condition was exacerbated by all the time he spent on horseback, maneuvering the American troops. Due to this, the great brigadier was forced to retire soon after the Battle of Cowpens, leading Greens "flying arming" to victory.

However, even after returning home from the battlefield, Morgan contributed to Patriot triumphs. One of his latest victories was stifling back the Pennsylvania Whiskey Rebellion, which was started by agitators in 1794. To honor his achievements as one the most resourceful and successful commanders of the American Revolution, Brigadier General Daniel Morgan received several recognitions.

In 1790, Morgan received a gold medal for his outstanding triumph at Cowpens. In 1797, he was appointed as a Federalist representative of Virginia in the United States House of Representatives. While he was planning to run for office two years later, his failing health prevented him from this. After this, he lived in his home in Winchester, Virginia, until his death in July 1802.

Chapter 9: Naval Warfare: John Paul Jones and the Bonhomme Richard

This chapter talks about American naval hero John Paul Jones, highlighting his background, experience, and contributions to the American Revolutionary War. It details how Jones was appointed to command the Bonhomme Richard and his challenges in building and leading a naval force. The chapter moves on to explain what led to the Battle of Flamborough Head and describes the epic duel between the Bonhomme Richard and the HMS Serapis. Besides highlighting key moments and tactical decisions made by John Paul Jones, it outlines Jones's leadership skills and determination in the wake of the most challenging moment of his naval career. Lastly, you'll learn about the impact of the Battle of Flamborough Head on naval tactics and strategy, both during the American Revolution and afterward.

Who Was John Paul Jones?

John Paul Jones joined the slave trade at 17 years old.
Rijksmuseum, CC0, via Wikimedia Commons:
https://commons.wikimedia.org/wiki/File:Portret_van_John_Paul_Jones,_RP-P-OB-62.519.jpg

John Paul Jones was born on July 6, 1747, in Kirkbean, Scotland. His father was the renowned gardener of Arbigland Estates. Only four of his many siblings and sisters survived to adulthood. His yearning for a life at sea was evident from an early age, and he went on to become a historical figure thanks to his dual legacy as a pirate and a naval hero. He liked to hang out at the adjacent port of Carsethorn despite his parents' best efforts to provide him with an appropriate education at the Kirkbean School. John Paul used to sneak down to the port whenever he had some free time and enjoyed hearing the sailors tell funny stories. He eventually made the decision to follow the call of the sea at the age of 12, starting an apprenticeship in the British Merchant Marine. John Paul was employed as a cabin boy by Scottish merchant shipper John Younger. John Paul quickly gave up his apprenticeship after sailing throughout the Americas and Barbados to join his brother, who later settled in Virginia and became a prosperous tailor.

When John Paul eventually made it back to Great Britain, he discovered that John Younger had lost interest in having him as an apprentice. John Paul, just 17 years old, soon discovered a different path and joined the slave trade aboard a brigantine. Due to his diligence, he was promoted to first mate and placed aboard the tiny ship Two Friends of Kingston, which was then based in Jamaica, in less than two years. John Paul traveled back and forth between Africa and the British Isles on multiple occasions before becoming disenchanted with the slave trade and going back to Scotland. The captain and first mate of the ship he took on his journey home passed away, and John Paul, who was well-suited to captain the ship—also named John—home, assumed command. At home, the owners of Kingston, the Two Friends, were so appreciative of his efforts to get the ship back safely that they appointed 21-year-old John Paul as captain.

John Paul started dressing and acting like a gentleman to live up to the land-popular fame of a captain, but he also occasionally lost his horrible fury. The latter caused him problems when he was charged with giving his ship's carpenter excessive beatings. The carpenter passed away from yellow fever; however, the first complaint against John Paul was dropped. Some speculated that this was because of his compromised state following the flogging. Following an announcement from the Barcelona Packet master, John Paul was released from custody and never faced the murder charge—though the accusation would eventually come back to haunt him.

After taking command of the ship <u>Betsy</u> in 1772, John Paul began a highly lucrative trading career, making numerous trips between Great Britain and the West Indies. However, after a mutiny broke out on his ship over a wage dispute, he was forced to kill the leader of the mutinous crew. Although he acted in self-defense, John Paul thought he would face the wrath of the man's family in the West Indies (and his previous accusation would only paint him in a bad light), so he fled to Virginia instead. He also changed his name to John Paul Jones to hide his identity as a British fugitive.

Upon hearing about the newly-sparked American Revolution, Jones quickly took to the rebels' side, sympathizing with their cause. When Congress established the Continental Navy, he felt his duty to go to Philadelphia and offer his expertise and skills. In December 1775, he was designated a first lieutenant in one of the Navy's handful of flagships... Alfred. It didn't take long for him to become a captain, albeit of another ship... the Providence. Traveling on this vessel, he reached the West Indies, where he began to mount his naval victories by defeating the British ship Glasgow. In 1776, he took to the Atlantic Ocean, sinking 8 ships, taking over another 8, and towing to port several more in less than a year.

Appointed as captain of a third ship, Ranger, in 1797, Jones continued with his raids on British home waters. However, his achievements weren't measured only by how much damage he caused to the British vessels. After arriving in Brest in May 1778, Jones was entrusted with the command of five more American and French ships. While he was already considered a hero at this point, he followed up by leading a successful cruise in the Irish Sea, defeating several smaller vessels – and to think his biggest achievement was yet to follow.

After being given the command of the ship Duc de Duras, he renamed it Bonhomme Richard (after Benjamin Franklin's alias, Poor Richard) and converted it into a veritable warship. It was on board this ship that he set sail to raid the commerce around the British shores... a voyage that placed him in the path of HMS Serapis and one of the most significant battles in naval history.

The Battle of Flamborough Head

When the Americans gained the French alliance after the Battle of Saratoga, the two countries also signed the Franco-American Treaty, which ensured that France would provide continued military assistance to the North American colonies. Beyond financing the Continental Army, this meant that from 1779, the French Navy would join in on the war against the British Royal Navy. By this time, John Paul Jones had already made a name for himself through his contributions to the naval patriot cause, including defeating HMS Drake in a battle in the North Channel, dividing Scotland and Ireland.

Now in possession of the Bonhomme Richard (a gift from the French Navy), Jones set sail from France to raid the English shores again on

August 14, 1779. He was accompanied by several smaller ships, including the Alliance, the Pallas, and the Vengeance. He continued his raids for a month, capturing several Scottish merchants and their vessels. As they headed north on the afternoon of September 23, 1779, Jones and his crew noticed an unidentified warship in their field of vision. Soon, the ship drew up its St. George's flag, so Jones instructed the Bonhomme Richard to display its striped American flag. Behind the unidentified vessel, several merchant ships became visible. As one attempted to escape the Alliance, the Pallas chased after it. However, since the Vengeance was further away, the Bonhomme Richard was left to confront the massive warship on its own.

The Bonhomme Richard was armed with six 18-pounders, fourteen 12-pounders, fourteen 9-pounders, and four 6-pounder cannons. Moreover, it was an old vessel built primarily for merchant purposes, and it was challenging to navigate quickly. This wasn't a problem against smaller ships, but it was when facing a much larger warship. By contrast, the identified vessel (which turned out to be the HMS Serapis, one of the British Navy's most prized warships, commanded by Captain Richard Pearson) was a 44-gun vessel, and on that day, it actually carried 50 cannons, ten 6-pounders, twenty 9-pounders, and twenty 18-pounders. On top of that, Jones's crew was severely reduced by recent deserters and crew members who were left behind or sent home on another ship after recently getting injured. Although Jones had also asked the captives he had on board to fight with him, few were willing to, so Jones only had a crew of 380, with the majority being young men or boys. 4 sailors and 15 marines, led by 24-year-old midshipman Nathaniel Fanning, were in charge of the maintop. The Mizzen top was occupied by 2 sailors, 6 marines, and one midshipman, while the foretops had 3 sailors, 10 marines, and a midshipman. There were another 20 marines in the rear deck, led by a French Army colonel. Meanwhile, the Serapis had a crew of 305, similarly assigned to different parts of the ship.

As he prepared for a battle, Jones ordered Fanning and the two young midshipmen (both were 16) to aim at the other ship's tops. They were to use small mortars, blunderbusses, muskets, and swivels – in other words, everything that could do as much damage as possible. This tactical move was to prevent the Serapis from using the British Navy's flagship move, firing at the enemy quarterdeck and incapacitating the crew. Just after 8 in the evening, Jones let the Serapis get closer, then ordered the Bonhomme Richard's courses changed, hoping to catch some wind. This prompted the Serapis to attack the American ship, igniting an epic battle that lasted for over 3 hours. In a broadside opening maneuver, the Serapis opened fire with its quarterdeck and upper deck weapons, causing significant damage to the Bonhomme Richards' starboard forward deck. Jones ordered the crew on their lower decks to discharge their cannons, but they seemed severely overmatched. Confident in an easy victory, the captain of the Serapis positioned his ship under the American vessel's stern and started to fire on it from his ship's side and top muskets, completely destroying the ensign staff, masts, and sails.

Jones's already short-staffed crew was further decimated, with some being forced to abandon their position and fight on other parts of the ship. The topmen, however, remained in their positions and continued to fire onto the British vessel's tops. Aware of his precarious position, Jones ordered the Bonhomme Richard to be turned around, hoping for a more favorable wind. As they were turning, the other vessel passed across their bow, and as the wind lifted the Bonhomme Richard's remaining sails, Jones ordered his ship to move forward as quickly as possible. As it was crossing the enemy's bow at a time, the Bonhomme Richard became entangled with the British vessel's starboard-side rigging and mizzen, trapping the Serapis. The captain of the Serapis attempted to extract his ship by setting the anchor and hoping to pull the vessel in that direction. However, as the two ships were connected, the force of the anchor hitting the water caused the American warship to rotate and latch both vessels in opposite directions, tethering them together. Jones promptly instructed his men to secure the Serapis with grappling irons, which the enemy crew attempted to cut off at first. However, eventually, there were so many grappling irons between the two ships that the Americans managed to pull the Serapis close alongside them. The crew of the Serapis tried to fight back by attacking the Bonhomme Richard's mizzenmast. Hoping to give his men time to regroup, the British captain tried to cut the American ship adrift. Meanwhile, the Bonhomme Richard's tops, now in a much more advantageous position, continued to attack and destroy the enemy's tops, with the last British topsmen being shot by Fanning himself.

While both ships still had their heaviest cannons, neither could use them because of the way the two vessels were tethered together. After a series of attacks and counterattacks with the smaller weapons, Jones' crew managed to clear the Serapis's decks. However, the British men from below were still continuing to fire at the Bonhomme Richard. An even bigger problem was that fire broke out on the Serapis, endangering both ships. For a short time, both parties ceased fire and proceeded to extinguish the flames that spread to both vessels. Jones's men were faster, and while the enemy was still occupied with their fire, they took possession of the Serapis' top platforms.

The Bonhomme Richard's topmen also seized control of the Serapis's forecastle, quarterdeck, and upper gun deck. However, the American vessel began sinking, and amid the chaos, the crewmen somehow thought that their captain and his officers were killed. Unsure of who was in charge, some of the surviving men wanted to surrender. When the British asked whether they were truly surrendering (striking colors, as known in naval circles), Jones emerged, declaring that he would rather sink, and so the fight continued. Another fire broke out, and it even spread to Fanning's maintop, but they managed to put it out. At this point, the fight was reduced to hand-to-hand combat, spiked with hand grenades, stinkpots, muskets, other guns, boarding axes, and pikes. While their maintop was almost impossible to control, the Serapis fired it once more, doing even more damage to the already half-sunk Bonhomme Richard. The captain of the Serapis then, once again, asked whether Jones would surrender, to which Jones replied, "I have not yet begun to fight!"

This was when the Alliance returned and immediately started firing at the Serapis. Unfortunately, because the two ships were too close, most of the damage was done to the Bonhomme Richard instead. Jones signaled the Alliance's captain, Pierre Landais, to cease fire, and he did (although he did intentionally fire at the Bonhomme Richard, thinking he could steal the victory from Jones by sinking his ship). After this, Jones ordered the release of the captives on board the Bonhomme Richard and asked them to fight alongside him, telling them that if they didn't save the ship, they would all lose their lives.

Somewhere around the third hour, Fanning's men threw a grenade at the Serapis' gun deck, which landed on loose gunpowder between the decks instead, causing a chain reaction upon its detonation. Now, it was the British crew who asked for quarters at the American ship, and Captain Pearson took down the ensign flag from its own ship. After almost four hours, the battle was over, and the crew of the Serapis surrendered. They all came to the Bonhomme Richard and surrendered their sidearms and swords, beginning with Captain Pearson, who also remarked that the Americans fought just as bravely as they did. Jones returned the compliment, ensuring Pearson that the Crown would surely recognize his courage and commend him for it.

After the Serapis surrendered, Jones inspected his own ship and found it in a dismayed condition. Seeing the amount of damage it sustained from the Serapis (and even the Alliance) and the nearly five feet of water that was now on board, Jones determined that the vessel couldn't be repaired and ordered his crew and the captives from the enemy vessel to board the Serapis instead. The Americans had 170 casualties, as opposed to the Brits, who lost 177 men.

The HSS Serapis sailed to Texel, Holland, where Jones released Pearson and his men. Jones even packed up the other captain's belongings and sent them after him, but Pearson refused to take them from the "rebel officer" (as the Brits viewed Americans) that Jones sent. However, he sent word that he would accept them from a French captain (as this was a nation officially recognized by Britain). Then, Jones asked the captain of Pallas, Denis Cotteneau, who was commissioned by the French king, to bring Pearson's belongings to him. This time, Pearson accepted the items graciously but, as Cotteneau noted, didn't thank him for their delivery because he knew the order came from Jones... an American.

Hearing Jones' incredible victory, the Dutch quickly named him "The Terror of the English." Later that year, Jones was given command of the HMS Serapis, which he renamed Serapis but didn't keep, gifting it to the French Navy as a prize ship instead.

In recognition of his achievements and the maintenance of freedom of the seas, Louis XVI of France bestowed upon Jones the rank of Chevalier, the Order of Military Merit, and a gold sword. This gesture, coupled with Jones's triumph over one of the largest vessels of the Royal British Navy, further solidified the French-American alliance, which ultimately secured the Americans the victory in their war for independence. Moreover, John Paul Jones' bravery and courage in the wake of an enormous disadvantage at the Battle of Flamborough Head inspired many other naval officers to fight just as hard, leading to victories like the one at the Siege of Yorktown in Virginia, two years later (which was coincidentally another French-American naval triumph). Due to his valor and maneuvering genius, Captain Jones has been aptly named the "Father of the American Navy."

After Congress passed a vote of gratitude for his contribution to the American Fleet, John Paul Jones was also given a gold medal in 1789. After returning to America in 1781, Jones spent years training naval officers and acting as an advisor for different naval establishments. However, when the Americans gained their victory and independence, Jones left these services and served as rear Admiral under Russian Empress Catherine II for two years. In 1790, he settled in Paris, where he remained until he died in 1792. Before his death, he wrote to his family members and also to the French Minister of Marine to ensure the men of the Bonhomme Richard would continue to receive their salaries.

Chapter 10: The Treaty of Paris: The Path to American Independence

In history, only a few documents have marked the birth of a nation as definitively as the Treaty of Paris. This venerable agreement, inked in the year 1783, stands as an enduring testament to the unyielding spirit of the American Revolution and the culmination of a remarkable journey toward independence. The Treaty of Paris was the instrument that brought an end to the hostilities between Great Britain and the thirteen rebellious American colonies. It was a document that held within its text the promise of a new and sovereign nation, the United States of America. It was a turning point in history, a testament to diplomacy and the enduring spirit of liberty, and a document that continues to shape the world in ways that its signatories could scarcely have imagined.

The signatories of the Treaty of Paris.
https://commons.wikimedia.org/wiki/File:Treaty_of_paris_1856.jpg

Early Diplomatic Initiatives

Amid the American Revolutionary War, diplomatic initiatives played a crucial role in setting the stage for formal peace negotiations. Two key events – the preliminary peace talks in Paris and the failed peace efforts in Staten Island, New York offer a nuanced view of the early attempts to find a diplomatic solution to the conflict.

1. **Preliminary Peace Talks in Paris**

    During the early stages of the war, several informal attempts were made to explore the possibility of peace. In 1776, Silas Deane, an American envoy, was sent to France to seek support and potentially negotiate peace. Deane's mission marked the first official step toward diplomacy in the European Theater.

    However, the notable preliminary peace talks occurred in Paris in 1778. The American delegation, consisting of Benjamin Franklin, Silas Deane, and Arthur Lee, engaged in discussions with British representatives. The British side was represented by Lord North's government. These initial talks were somewhat exploratory in nature and did not lead to concrete results, but they set the stage for future negotiations.

The American delegation was at a diplomatic disadvantage, as they had not yet achieved significant military victories, and Britain did not formally recognize the independence of the United States. Despite these challenges, these early conversations in Paris marked a significant milestone, as they demonstrated a willingness on both sides to engage in diplomatic efforts, even if they were inconclusive at the time.

2. **Failed Peace Efforts in Staten Island, New York, in 1776**

In the summer of 1776, during the early years of the American Revolution, there were attempts to initiate peace talks on Staten Island, New York. This effort emerged when Admiral Lord Richard Howe and General William Howe, British military commanders, were authorized to negotiate with the American Continental Congress.

The Howes were empowered to offer pardons to those who would lay down their arms and were seen as an early overture toward reconciliation. They met with John Adams, Benjamin Franklin, and Edward Rutledge, who were acting on behalf of the Continental Congress.

However, these peace talks ultimately failed to yield a lasting agreement. The primary reason was the British refusal to recognize American independence. Instead, they sought a return to British rule, which the American representatives could not accept.

The stalemate in Staten Island was an early indication of the fundamental differences between the American and British positions. While there were talks, they did not lead to a peaceful resolution. The conflict would continue for several more years until the conditions were right for the negotiations that ultimately resulted in the Treaty of Paris.

These early diplomatic initiatives revealed the complexities and challenges of negotiating a peace settlement during a protracted conflict. While they did not immediately lead to peace, they laid the groundwork for future negotiations, marking the beginning of a diplomatic process that would eventually conclude with the recognition of American independence in the Treaty of Paris in 1783.

The American Delegation

The American delegation that represented the interests of the United States in the negotiations leading up to the Treaty of Paris included several notable figures, each of whom brought a unique set of skills, experiences, and contributions to the peace process.

1. **Benjamin Franklin**

    Benjamin Franklin, a renowned polymath, scientist, and statesman, was one of the most influential American diplomats during this period. He brought considerable diplomatic experience to the table, having previously served as an American envoy in France. His charm and wit made him an effective negotiator. His reputation preceded him, as he was well-known and respected in European intellectual and political circles. Franklin's role in securing French support for the American cause was instrumental in the success of the negotiations.

2. **John Adams**

    John Adams, a lawyer, political theorist, and one of the Founding Fathers, was known for his intellectual rigor and staunch commitment to American independence. Adams was highly knowledgeable about political philosophy and legal matters, and his legal background made him an astute negotiator. His dedication to the cause of independence and his commitment to American principles were invaluable in advancing American interests during the negotiations.

3. **John Jay**

    John Jay, a diplomat, lawyer, and statesman, was another key member of the American delegation. He brought legal expertise and diplomatic experience to the negotiations. Jay would go on to have a significant role in crafting the Treaty of Paris, particularly concerning the boundary disputes and other legal aspects of the treaty. His pragmatism and attention to detail were crucial to the success of the negotiations.

The British Delegation and Their Perspectives

On the British side, the delegation tasked with negotiating with the former American colonies faced a complex set of challenges, both in terms of their composition and their overall perspective.

British Delegation Members

The British delegation was led by individuals like Richard Oswald, a former Member of Parliament with a background in trade, and David Hartley, a seasoned diplomat. Lord Shelburne, the British Prime Minister at the time, played a significant role in authorizing and guiding the negotiation process. These figures were more experienced in trade and diplomacy rather than the military, and they were tasked with a difficult mission: to negotiate with their former colonists.

Reservations about Negotiating

The British delegation's reservations about negotiating with the former colonists were deeply rooted in the political and social context of the time. In Britain, there were varying opinions about the American situation. Some saw the American colonies as an important part of the British Empire and were reluctant to grant them independence. Others believed that the war had become costly and unwinnable.

Public opinion in Britain was divided, with some expressing a desire to continue the war and others favoring reconciliation. The political landscape was also complicated, with differing views within the British government on how to handle the American situation.

Initial Demands and Expectations

During the negotiations that preceded the Treaty of Paris, both the American and British delegations had distinct demands and expectations that reflected their respective positions and concerns.

American Delegations' Demands and Expectations

1. **Recognition of Independence**

    The foremost and non-negotiable demand of the American delegation was the formal recognition of American independence from Great Britain. This was the ultimate goal of the American Revolution, and it lay at the core of their demands. The American representatives were steadfast in their commitment to achieving full sovereignty and autonomy for the United States.

2. **Territorial Boundaries**

    The American delegation sought to establish clear and favorable territorial boundaries for the new nation. The negotiations aimed to define the extent of American territory, which would encompass vast lands extending westward to the Mississippi River. The negotiations would address how far west the new nation's borders would extend.

3. **Fishing Rights**

The American delegation had a keen interest in securing fishing rights, particularly in the North Atlantic. This included the right to fish off the Grand Banks of Newfoundland, which was a vital area for American fishermen. Access to these fishing grounds was essential for the economic prosperity of coastal communities in New England.

British Demands and Expectations

1. **Protect Loyalist Interests**

The British delegation was concerned with safeguarding the interests of Loyalists who had remained loyal to the Crown during the Revolutionary War. They sought to ensure that these individuals would not face persecution or loss of property after American independence was established. The fate of Loyalists was a central issue, as the British wanted to secure their protection and well-being.

2. **Retain Certain Territories**

The British were reluctant to cede all the territory they held in North America. Specifically, they aimed to retain strategic posts and territories that held military and economic value. For example, they wanted to hold on to Quebec and Newfoundland while possibly maintaining control over the Great Lakes region. The negotiation of territorial boundaries would be a critical point of contention.

Key Issues Addressed During Negotiations

As the American and British delegations engaged in the negotiations leading up to the Treaty of Paris, several key issues took center stage, reflecting the complex and multifaceted nature of the settlement.

Negotiation of Territorial Boundaries

One of the central issues addressed during the negotiations was the determination of the new boundaries of the United States. The American delegation aimed to secure vast territorial claims that extended westward to the Mississippi River, which would encompass much of the

Ohio Valley and the region known as the Old Northwest. The British, however, sought to retain certain strategic territories, which led to extensive discussions about where these boundaries would be drawn.

Fishing Rights

Fishing rights were a critical economic concern for both sides, particularly for the American delegation. American fishermen relied on access to the rich fishing grounds off the Grand Banks of Newfoundland. The negotiations focused on the extent to which American fishermen would have access to these valuable waters.

Treatment of Loyalists

The fate of Loyalists, those who had remained loyal to the British Crown during the war, was another contentious issue. The British delegation insisted on protecting Loyalist interests and ensuring they would not face persecution or loss of property in the newly independent United States. The American delegation was hesitant to make strong concessions on this issue, as they were concerned about granting privileges to those who had supported the British cause.

Role of the Mississippi River and the Great Lakes

The Mississippi River and the Great Lakes played pivotal roles in defining the new boundaries of the United States. The inclusion of the Mississippi River as the western boundary was crucial for American interests, as it opened up vast lands for westward expansion. Additionally, the control of the Great Lakes region was a point of contention. The British had established military posts and maintained a presence in the Great Lakes area, and their evacuation and the delineation of the new boundary would be a major focus of the negotiations.

The Mississippi River, in particular, was a significant geographical feature, and its inclusion as the western boundary of the United States allowed for access to the river and facilitated trade and westward expansion. The Great Lakes, on the other hand, held military, economic, and strategic importance, and their control had implications for the security and commerce of the region.

Formal Recognition of American Independence

The central provision of the Treaty of Paris, signed on September 3, 1783, was the formal recognition of American independence by Great Britain. This pivotal recognition had profound implications both within the newly established United States and on the international stage.

Central Provision of the Treaty of Paris

The Treaty of Paris solidified the end of the American Revolutionary War and officially acknowledged the sovereignty of the United States of America. The treaty explicitly stated that Great Britain recognized the United States as an independent and sovereign nation, free from British rule and authority.

Significance in a National Context

The formal recognition of independence in the United States was an exultant moment, marking the fulfillment of the revolutionaries' ardent desires and struggles. It validated the sacrifices made during the war and the vision of a self-governing nation. The recognition of American independence laid the foundation for the development of a new form of government and the establishment of the principles and values enshrined in the United States' founding documents, such as the Declaration of Independence and the Constitution.

Significance in an International Context

Internationally, the recognition of American independence had far-reaching consequences. It signaled the emergence of the United States as a sovereign entity on the global stage. This newfound nation entered the community of nations with the legitimacy and respect that formal recognition bestowed. The Treaty of Paris set a precedent for other colonial nations striving for independence, and it reshaped the world order by contributing to the decline of colonial empires.

Moreover, the recognition of American independence had diplomatic and economic implications. It opened the door to diplomatic relations and treaties with other nations. The United States, unburdened by British colonial regulations, was now free to engage in trade and establish alliances with foreign powers. This had a significant impact on the nation's future economic and political relationships.

The Treaty of Paris was a clear indication of the changing dynamics in the world, with the former colony successfully challenging a global superpower and achieving recognition as a fully sovereign state. It encouraged the spread of democratic ideals and the belief in self-determination, influencing the development of international relations and the course of history.

Ratification Process

The ratification process of the Treaty of Paris, both in the United States and Great Britain, was a crucial phase following the negotiation of the treaty. It was marked by a series of debates, challenges, and political reactions on both sides of the Atlantic.

Ratification in the United States

In the United States, the ratification process was conducted by the Continental Congress, the governing body of the newly formed nation. The Treaty of Paris was a pivotal document, as it would determine the terms of peace and the country's international standing.

The ratification process in the Continental Congress was not without challenges. There were debates and differences of opinion among delegates from different states. Some Congress members were concerned about the terms of the treaty, especially the treatment of Loyalists and territorial boundaries. Additionally, there were concerns about whether the treaty would fully safeguard American interests.

Ultimately, the Treaty of Paris was ratified by the Continental Congress on January 14, 1784, and the United States officially became a party to the treaty. The successful ratification in the United States marked the formal acceptance of the terms of peace and paved the way for the nation to emerge as a sovereign entity on the world stage.

Ratification in Great Britain

In Great Britain, the ratification process also carried its own set of political and public reactions. The British government, led by Prime Minister William Pitt the Younger, was tasked with securing the ratification of the treaty.

The ratification process in Great Britain was influenced by political divisions. Some factions believed that the war had become too costly and unsustainable, and it was in the best interest of the nation to acknowledge American independence. Others, however, were deeply opposed to the idea of recognizing American sovereignty.

The general public in Britain also had mixed opinions about the treaty. While some advocated for ending the war and recognizing American independence, others viewed it as a national humiliation. The idea of acknowledging the independence of former colonists was met with resistance by many.

Ultimately, the Treaty of Paris was ratified by the British Parliament on April 9, 1784. This formalized the recognition of American independence and marked the end of the hostilities between the two nations. The British government's decision to ratify the treaty reflected the prevailing sentiment that continuing the war was no longer feasible, and it was time to bring an end to the costly conflict.

Post-War Relations

The Treaty of Paris marked the formal end of hostilities and the beginning of a new phase in the relationship between the United States and Great Britain. While it was a clear recognition of American independence, it did not immediately resolve all issues or disputes between the two nations.

The treaty set the stage for future diplomacy and trade between the United States and Great Britain. Diplomatic relations were established, and the countries began to negotiate various agreements to address issues such as trade and boundaries.

Over time, the relationship evolved, and tensions between the United States and Great Britain persisted, leading to conflicts such as the War of 1812. However, the treaty's recognition of American independence laid the foundation for developing a more normalized relationship between the two nations in the following years and decades.

In conclusion, the Treaty of Paris had profound consequences for the United States, including significant territorial gains, secure fishing rights, and the mixed fate of Loyalists. It also marked the beginning of a new chapter in the post-war relations between the United States and Great Britain, ultimately influencing the trajectory of American expansion and its evolving position on the world stage. The treaty's recognition of American sovereignty was a transformative moment in history, setting the United States on a path of nation-building and global engagement.

Conclusion

The American Revolution was one of the most influential events in American history. It showed the strength, patriotism, and courage of the American people, which led to their victory. There were also tales about traitors, spies, and trickery. Everything that took place at the time shaped America and turned it into the country it is today.

You started your journey by learning about early American leaders and how they established a network of spies to gather intelligence about the British. You then explored the role of Benjamin Tallmadge as chief organizer of the Culper Spy Ring and his relationship with George Washington. You also learned about the main operatives in the ring and their methods and techniques.

You then discovered the interesting history of guerrilla warfare and how Francis Marion used this tactic to slow down the British, which contributed to the Americans' victory. You also discovered American heroine Deborah Sampson and the great lengths she went through to serve her country.

There are many interesting details about the Revolutionary War, like the challenging winter in 1777-1778. You discovered how the severe weather conditions affected the troops and the stories about their bravery and resilience.

The British defeat in the Battle of Saratoga sparked some of the biggest events in the Revolutionary War. You learned how the North's victory led to the alliance with the French and the British departure from the North to head south.

Native American tribes played a major role in the war. You saw how some of them were loyal to the Americans while others betrayed them and pledged their allegiance to the British.

Benedict Arnold is one of the most popular figures in the Revolutionary War. You learned everything about his life, from his military success to all the struggles he faced, leading to his betrayal.

You also discovered the strategic importance of the Southern Theater and the American and British key figures in the South. You learned about naval commander John Paul Jones and his role in the Battle of Flamborough Head. You finished your journey with the battles that led to the peace treaty in Paris between the British and the Americans.

The Revolutionary War was the biggest movement of any nation in modern history. The Americans inspired the world and showed them that they could gain their independence if they came together and fought for their country. This historic event created a country that prides itself on its civil rights, equality, and liberty.

Each of the tales told here aims to paint an illustrative picture of the American Revolution and its legacy on its people and on the world.

Check out another book in the series

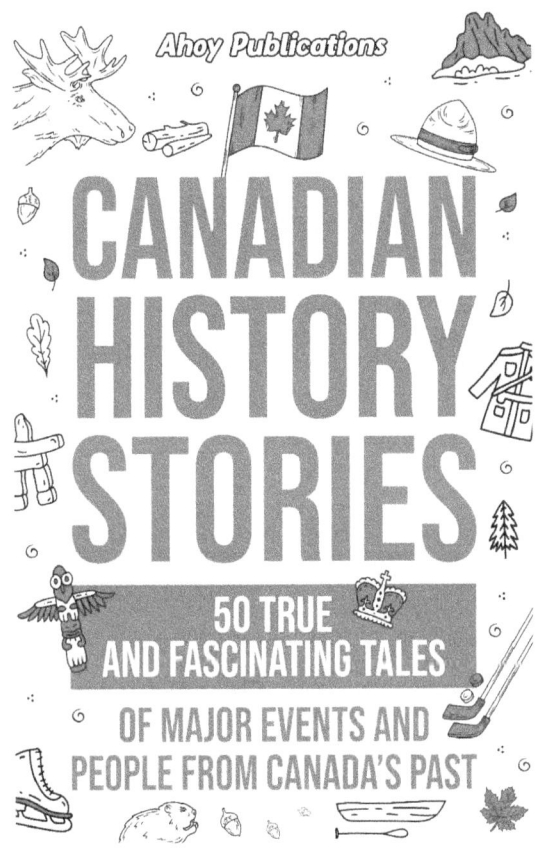

References

(N.d.). Amrevmuseum.org. https://www.amrevmuseum.org/5-pop-culture-portrayals-of-benedict-arnold#:~:text=Benedict%20Arnold's%20journey%20from%20a,culture%20in%20the%20United%20States.

(N.d.-a). Loc.gov. https://www.loc.gov/classroom-materials/united-states-history-primary-source-timeline/civil-war-and-reconstruction-1861-1877/south-during-the-civil-war/

(N.d.-b). Loc.gov. https://www.loc.gov/classroom-materials/united-states-history-primary-source-timeline/american-revolution-1763-1783/revolutionary-war-southern-phase-1778-1781/

Allison, S. (2015, May 17). Deborah Sampson: A patriot by any other name. Heroes: What They Do & Why We Need Them. https://blog.richmond.edu/heroes/2015/05/17/deborah-sampson-a-patriot-by-any-other-name/

Ambush: Francis Marion and the art of guerrilla warfare. (2021, April 20). American Battlefield Trust. https://www.battlefields.org/learn/articles/ambush-francis-marion-and-art-guerrilla-warfare

American Revolution in the Mohawk Valley. (n.d.). https://www.mohawkvalleyhistory.com/themes/revolutionary-war

American Revolutionary War - Heroes Stories. (2020, February 25). Home of Heroes. https://homeofheroes.com/heroes-stories/american-revolutionary-war/

Andrews, E. (2016, January 13). 9 things you may not know about Benedict Arnold. HISTORY. https://www.history.com/news/9-things-you-may-not-know-about-benedict-arnold

Battle of Cowpens. (2009, November 9). HISTORY. https://www.history.com/topics/american-revolution/battle-of-cowpens

Battle of Quebec 1775: Date & American Revolution. (2009, November 2). HISTORY. https://www.history.com/topics/american-revolution/battle-of-quebec-1775

Battle of Saratoga. (2009, November 13). HISTORY. https://www.history.com/topics/american-revolution/battle-of-saratoga

Battle of Saratoga. (n.d.). George Washington's Mount Vernon. https://www.mountvernon.org/library/digitalhistory/digital-encyclopedia/article/battle-of-saratoga/

Benedict Arnold commits treason. (2009, November 24). HISTORY. https://www.history.com/this-day-in-history/benedict-arnold-commits-treason

Benedict Arnold fights valiantly at Valcour Island. (2009, November 13). HISTORY. https://www.history.com/this-day-in-history/benedict-arnold-fights-valiantly-at-valcour-island

Benedict Arnold. (2009, October 27). HISTORY. https://www.history.com/topics/american-revolution/benedict-arnold

Benedict Arnold. (n.d.-a). George Washington's Mount Vernon. https://www.mountvernon.org/george-washington/the-revolutionary-war/george-washington-benedict-arnold/benedict-arnold/

Benedict Arnold. (n.d.-b). American Battlefield Trust. https://www.battlefields.org/learn/biographies/benedict-arnold

Benedict Arnold. (n.d.-c). Ushistory.org. https://www.ushistory.org/valleyforge/served/arnold.html

Bluhm, R. K. (2017). Battle of Long Island. In Encyclopedia Britannica.

Boston Tea Party Ships & Museum. (2019, September 24). American Revolution. Boston Tea Party Ships; Boston Tea Party Ships & Museum. https://www.bostonteapartyship.com/american-revolution

Bradford, W., Washington, G., & River, H. (n.d.). Sampson, Deborah. Encyclopedia.com. https://www.encyclopedia.com/history/educational-magazines/sampson-deborah

British occupation of New York City. (n.d.). George Washington's Mount Vernon. https://www.mountvernon.org/library/digitalhistory/digital-encyclopedia/article/british-occupation-of-new-york-city/

Bryan, A. (2023, September 5). The Treaty of Paris: The American negotiators. Teaching American History; TeachingAmericanHistory.org. https://teachingamericanhistory.org/blog/the-treaty-of-paris-the-american-negotiators/

Cowpens. (n.d.). American Battlefield Trust. https://www.battlefields.org/learn/revolutionary-war/battles/cowpens

Daniel Morgan. (n.d.). American Battlefield Trust. https://www.battlefields.org/learn/biographies/daniel-morgan

Daniel Morgan. (n.d.). George Washington's Mount Vernon. https://www.mountvernon.org/library/digitalhistory/digital-encyclopedia/article/daniel-morgan/

Deborah Sampson. (n.d.-a). American Battlefield Trust. https://www.battlefields.org/learn/biographies/deborah-sampson

Deborah Sampson. (n.d.-b). George Washington's Mount Vernon. https://www.mountvernon.org/library/digitalhistory/digital-encyclopedia/article/deborah-sampson/

Deborah Sampson: American Revolutionary War Hero. (n.d.). Mass.gov. https://www.mass.gov/info-details/deborah-sampson-american-revolutionary-war-hero

Deborah Sampson: American warrior. (n.d.). Libertyfund.org. https://oll.libertyfund.org/reading-room/2022-10-11-deborah-sampson-american-warrior

Deborah Sampson's legacy. (2020, March 16). U.S. Senator John Boozman. https://www.boozman.senate.gov/public/index.cfm/2020/3/deborah-sampson-s-legacy

Delaney Lust Davis High School. (2017, March 26). Women in History: Revolutionary War fighter Deborah Sampson hid her gender for years. Yakima Herald-Republic. https://www.yakimaherald.com/unleashed/women-in-history-revolutionary-war-fighter-deborah-sampson-hid-her-gender-for-years/article_60e4911c-11e0-11e7-b036-5f061300753f.html

Diana. (2017, March 1). Deborah Sampson, U.S. Army. Foundation for Women Warriors. https://foundationforwomenwarriors.org/deborah-sampson-u-s-army/

Digital History. (n.d.). Digitalhistory.uh.edu. https://www.digitalhistory.uh.edu/era.cfm?eraid=3&smtid=1

Espionage tactics. (n.d.). George Washington's Mount Vernon. https://www.mountvernon.org/library/digitalhistory/digital-encyclopedia/article/espionage-tactics/

France in the American Revolution. (2021, January 6). American Battlefield Trust. https://www.battlefields.org/learn/articles/france-american-revolution

George Washington's Mount Vernon. (n.d.). Loyalists. https://www.mountvernon.org/library/digitalhistory/digital-encyclopedia/article/loyalists/

Gould, K. (2023). Culper Spy Ring. In Encyclopedia Britannica.

Guerrilla warfare. (2013, June 3). American Battlefield Trust. https://www.battlefields.org/learn/articles/guerrilla-warfare

Hand, T. (2023, January 31). A desperate winter at Valley Forge. Americana Corner. https://www.americanacorner.com/blog/valley-forge

Hickman, K. (2011, January 25). American revolution brigadier General Francis Marion (The Swamp Fox). ThoughtCo. https://www.thoughtco.com/brigadier-general-francis-marion-swamp-fox-2360605

Historical, S. (n.d.). The story of Deborah Sampson, woman soldier of the revolution. Samson Historical. https://www.samsonhistorical.com/blogs/reliving-history/deborah-sampson

Jaenen, C. J. (n.d.). Treaty of Paris 1783. Thecanadianencyclopedia.Ca. https://www.thecanadianencyclopedia.ca/en/article/treaty-of-paris-1783

John Paul Jones. (n.d.). American Battlefield Trust. https://www.battlefields.org/learn/biographies/john-paul-jones

John Paul Jones. (n.d.). Nhhcaws.Local.

Katz, B. (2019, July 2). Diary sheds light on Deborah Sampson, who fought in the Revolutionary War. Smithsonian Magazine. https://www.smithsonianmag.com/smart-news/diary-sheds-light-deborah-sampson-who-fought-revolutionary-war-180972547/

Khandelwal, P. (2020, February 14). Francis Marion. Revolutionary War. https://www.revolutionary-war.net/francis-marion/

Klein, C. (2021, September 8). How the South Helped Win the American Revolution. HISTORY. https://www.history.com/news/american-revolution-southern-battles/

Klein, C. (2022, September 15). West Point's critical role in the American Revolution. HISTORY. https://www.history.com/news/west-point-fort-revolutionary-war

Kowalski, H. (2021, December 14). Bidwell Lore - Deborah Sampson: Revolutionary soldier and revolutionary woman. Bidwell House Museum. https://www.bidwellhousemuseum.org/blog/2021/12/14/bidwell-lore-deborah-sampson-revolutionary-soldier-and-revolutionary-woman/

Lohnes, K. (2023). Battles of Saratoga. In Encyclopedia Britannica.

Milestones: 1776-1783 - office of the historian. (n.d.). State.gov. https://history.state.gov/milestones/1776-1783/french-alliance

Milestones: 1776-1783 - office of the historian. (n.d.). State.gov. https://history.state.gov/milestones/1776-1783/treaty

Mohawk River – Oregon Conservation Strategy. (n.d.). https://www.oregonconservationstrategy.org/conservation-opportunity-area/mohawk-river/

Mohawk Valley Region | Cooperstown | Saratoga | Leatherstocking. (n.d.). https://www.mohawkvalleyhistory.com/about/region

Mohawk Valley: Early St. Johnsville Pioneers | National Postal Museum. (n.d.). https://postalmuseum.si.edu/exhibition/indians-at-the-post-office-murals-encounter/mohawk-valley-early-st-johnsville-pioneers

Nathan Hale: American patriot. Army ranger. Spy. (n.d.). Cia.gov. https://www.cia.gov/stories/story/nathan-hale-american-patriot-army-ranger-spy/

Norton, L. A. (2019, August 20). The Battle between Bonhomme Richard and Serapis. Journal of the American Revolution. https://allthingsliberty.com/2019/08/the-battle-between-bonhomme-richard-and-serapis/

Office of the Director of National Intelligence. (n.d.). INTEL - Culper spy ring. Intel.gov. https://www.intel.gov/evolution-of-espionage/revolutionary-war/culper-spy-ring

Office of the Director of National Intelligence. (n.d.). INTEL - Benedict Arnold. Intel.gov. https://www.intel.gov/evolution-of-espionage/revolutionary-war/british-espionage/benedict-arnold

Office of the Director of National Intelligence. (n.d.). INTEL - Benedict Arnold. Intel.gov. https://www.intel.gov/evolution-of-espionage/revolutionary-war/british-espionage/benedict-arnold

Oriskany. (n.d.). American Battlefield Trust. https://www.battlefields.org/learn/revolutionary-war/battles/oriskany

Overview of the American Revolutionary War. (2017, January 26). American Battlefield Trust. https://www.battlefields.org/learn/articles/overview-american-revolutionary-war

Philbrick, N. (2016, April 20). Why Benedict Arnold turned traitor against the American Revolution. Smithsonian Magazine. https://www.smithsonianmag.com/history/benedict-arnold-turned-traitor-american-revolution-180958786/

Read: Who is Deborah Sampson? (2017, April 14). IAVA. https://iava.org/blog/who-is-deborah-sampson/

Records reveal an overlooked hero of the Culper spy ring. (2022, November 7). New York Almanack. https://www.newyorkalmanack.com/2022/11/records-reveal-overlooked-hero-of-culper-spy-ring/

Remembering a Women's rights pioneer: Deborah Sampson. (n.d.). Fairchild Air Force Base.

https://www.fairchild.af.mil/News/Commentaries/Display/Article/496443/remembering-a-womens-rights-pioneer-deborah-sampson/

Revolutionary War. (2009, October 29). HISTORY. https://www.history.com/topics/american-revolution/american-revolution-history

Salomonsson, R. (2006, June 27). Women of the revolution: Deborah Sampson. Christian Science Monitor (Boston, Mass.: 1983). https://www.csmonitor.com/2006/0627/p18s03-hfks.html

Saratoga. (n.d.). American Battlefield Trust. https://www.battlefields.org/learn/revolutionary-war/battles/saratoga

Seven, J. (2018, July 17). Why did Benedict Arnold betray America? HISTORY. https://www.history.com/news/why-did-benedict-arnold-betray-america

Shippen, P. (2014, April 3). Benedict Arnold. Biography. https://www.biography.com/military-figures/benedict-arnold

Southern theater of the American Revolutionary War. (n.d.). American Revolutionary War Wiki; Fandom, Inc. https://arw.fandom.com/wiki/Southern_theater_of_the_American_Revolutionary_War

The Battle of Flamborough Head. (2021, July 15). American Battlefield Trust. https://www.battlefields.org/learn/articles/battle-flamborough-head

The Culper Spy Ring. (2010, March 19). HISTORY. https://www.history.com/topics/american-revolution/culper-spy-ring

The Editors of Encyclopaedia Britannica. (1998a, July 20). Battle of Oriskany | Revolutionary War, Mohawk Valley, Patriot Victory. Encyclopedia Britannica. https://www.britannica.com/event/Battle-of-Oriskany

The Editors of Encyclopaedia Britannica. (1998b, July 20). Quartering Act | Summary, Significance, & Facts. Encyclopedia Britannica. https://www.britannica.com/event/Quartering-Act

The Editors of Encyclopedia Britannica. (2023). New England. In Encyclopedia Britannica.

The Erie Canal. (n.d.). https://www.eriecanal.org/

The Southern Theater of the American Revolution. (2017, January 26). American Battlefield Trust. https://www.battlefields.org/learn/articles/southern-theater-american-revolution

The Southern Theater of the American Revolution. (2017, January 26). American Battlefield Trust. https://www.battlefields.org/learn/articles/southern-theater-american-revolution

The Treaty of Paris. (2019, August 2). American Battlefield Trust. https://www.battlefields.org/learn/articles/treaty-paris

The United States Army - WWII, Korean War, Cold War. (n.d.). In Encyclopedia Britannica.

Treaty of Paris (1783). (2021, April 16). National Archives. https://www.archives.gov/milestone-documents/treaty-of-paris

Treaty of Paris. (2009, November 13). HISTORY. https://www.history.com/topics/american-revolution/treaty-of-paris

Valley Forge. (2018, December 12). HISTORY. https://www.history.com/topics/american-revolution/valley-forge

Wallace, W. M. (2023). American Revolution. In Encyclopedia Britannica.

Washington's winters. (n.d.). George Washington's Mount Vernon. https://www.mountvernon.org/george-washington/so-hard-a-winter/

What happened at Valley Forge - Valley Forge National Historical Park (U.S. National Park service). (n.d.). Nps.gov. https://www.nps.gov/vafo/learn/historyculture/valley-forge-history-and-significance.htm

What type of warfare did Francis Marion and his men employ? (n.d.). Socratic.org. https://socratic.org/questions/what-type-of-warfare-did-francis-marion-and-his-men-employ

Why Francis Marion became the father of guerrilla warfare. (2020, January 28). Warfare History Network. https://warfarehistorynetwork.com/article/why-francis-marion-became-the-father-of-guerrilla-warfare/

Winter at Valley Forge. (2017, September 21). American Battlefield Trust. https://www.battlefields.org/learn/articles/winter-valley-forge